An Attitude and Approach

for Teaching Music to Special Learners

An Attitude and Approach

for Teaching Music to Special Learners

Elise S. Sobol

Pentland Press, Inc.
www.pentlandpressusa.com

PUBLISHED BY PENTLAND PRESS, INC.
5122 Bur Oak Circle, Raleigh, North Carolina 27612
United States of America
919-782-0281

ISBN 1-57197-296-X
Library of Congress Control Number: 2001 132266

Printed in China

"This is a book that must be read by **every music teacher—** whether you are a college music education major, or a 50-year teaching veteran. Although the book is aimed primarily toward "special learners" it is really applicable to **all learners,** for all children are "special." This book clearly defines the various definitions and types of disabilities, and it offers positive strategies for implementing new programs and concepts into the music classroom. Congratulations, Elise—we've been needing this book for a long time!"

Elaine L. Gates
President, NYS Council of Music Teacher Education Programs
Director, Undergraduate Music Education, New York University

"It gives me a great deal of pleasure to write in support of Elise Sobol's comprehensive book, *An Attitude and Approach for Teaching Music to Special Learners.* This book is for all music educators. It is both a philosophy and a "how to" book with a wealth of information. I believe it is essential for all educators and as such should be added to everyone's reference materials. It is based on a sound and logical approach to teaching by a master teacher who is innovative, resourceful, and caring, with years of experience in the field."

Peter Brasch
Chairperson, Council of Music Education Associations
Past President, New York State School Music Association
Coordinator of Music, Commack Public Schools, Retired

To my sons, Marlon and Aaron Sobol

With love, forever and always

Table of Contents

Foreword

I first had the great pleasure of meeting Elise Sobol when she attended the Twenty-Sixth International Congress on Arts and Communications in Lisbon, Portugal in July 1999. I was hosting the Congress as Director General of the International Biographical Centre from Cambridge in England. As if it were yesterday I remember her piano recital as part of the Concert Evening and the following morning I, along with the other delegates who were attending her talk, was spellbound by her eloquence and art of communication. Elise talks TO her listeners, not AT them. From the enthusiasm and feedback that she generates from her audience I would imagine that this applies to listeners of all ages and abilities. Incidentally, the full text of her speech is featured in this book and I would urge any reader or researcher to study it and its successors that were delivered at the Twenty-Seventh International Congress in Washington, D.C. and at the latest Congress last month at Cambridge University in England. Elise Sobol has this year deservedly been made a professor in the Department of Music and the Performing Arts Professions at New York University. She is also a highly respected special needs music teacher at the Nassau Boces Jerusalem Avenue Elementary Program. She is listed in numerous international biographical reference publications and as her reputation spreads she will no doubt receive even more international acclaim with the publication of this, her first major publication, *An Attitude and Approach for Teaching Music to Special Learners.* She will undoubtedly go on to write other works in this and perhaps other fields, but I commend this book to you not only for its scholarly content but also for the fact that it is simply just a very good and interesting read. Enough from me but I conclude with the verbatim words from one of Elise's learning disabled students, Isaac Robinson who, when asked the question,

"Who would you look up to as a hero or heroine?" wrote: "She is the music teacher here. I look up to Ms. Sobol . . . she ask me to get on the drums and she said I was good, after that I play . . . and I play . . . and I play."

NICHOLAS S. LAW
Director General of the International Biographical Centre
Cambridge, England, August, 2001

Preface

It is with pleasure that this informative book, based on my years of experience as an early childhood, regular and special education music teacher, college professor and guest speaker both here and abroad, is published by Pentland Press. Teaching is a commitment so much more than a profession. It is a commitment to the belief that each child is unique and completely whole, no matter what challenges the child faces. It is a commitment to the belief that each child is here to make a contribution with his or her life and that through music, children can communicate and gain skills for academic achievement, social, emotional, and psychological well-being. Foundations of music education for teaching special learners include a teacher's love of children, understanding those with special needs, training, skill, and presentation of materials through a reality-based system which uses multisensory techniques. The success of this approach is further defined with active patience and belief in the positive and the possible. *An Attitude and Approach for Teaching Music to Special Learners* was developed in large part through my service work as New York State School Music Chairperson for Special Learners. It is intended to be a resource for the mind and the spirit—a handbook to bring a joy of music and life success for students of all ages and learning styles.

Acknowledgements

I acknowledge with sincere thanks the hundreds and hundreds of special children that I have had the pleasure of teaching. They have blessed me with their winning spirit and in so doing have lit the way for my attitude and approach for teaching music to special learners. In addition, I extend my gratitude to the following people who have helped me nurture my experience, talents and gifts in public service to music education: Joseph and Clara Sugar for their profound leadership and recommendation to serve as Chairperson under past NYSSMA presidents Peter Brasch, William Mercer, Richard Rabideau, Earl Groner and with association colleagues; Dr. Edward Marschilok, New York State Education Department; my present and past administrators at the Board of Cooperative Educational Services of Nassau County for their professional guidance—Patricia Busset, Frank Barrett, Barbara Longo, Amy Goldstein, Joanne Nelson, the late Bonnie Klingerman, Ronnie Funk and Dr. Herbert Feingold; Orff-Schulwerk mentor, Joan Fretz; singer/songwriter Janice Buckner for her inspiration and for her collaborations with me in performing with children who have severe disabilities; her husband Dr. Richard Statler whose work introduced me to the many levels of sound healing; to Jeanmarie Colquhoun for her genuine friendship and artistic guidance; Anita Gelber for her candid honesty throughout the many facets of my career; to the many family members and friends who have contributed towards my positive outlook of all life's challenges; and to the American Biographical Institute (USA) and the International Biographical Centre (UK), who have extended through their publications and jointly sponsored International Congresses worldwide recognition for my contributions to society in the fields of special music education and performance.

The Basics

AEIOU's of Teaching Special Learners

The music room should be a happy place where all students feel safe, secure, and successful.

A—Assurance
E—Esteem
I —Interaction
O—Opportunity
U—Understanding
_____

Y—You

ABC's of Vocal and Instrumental Adaptation

I. Vocal adaptation

    A. Use songs with limited range

    B. Use songs with a lot of repetition

    C. Use songs that can be easily memorized

II. Instrumental adaptation

    A. Use tactile aids for string and wind instruments

    B. Use visual aids for keyboard identification

    C. Use color coding for percussion

          high—middle—low

Classroom Set-Up

In setting up your music classroom, keep in mind that all students need to feel equal. There should be no front or back rows; rather, a horseshoe formation for chairs, with direct access to entrance and exit door, instrument closets, audio equipment, etc. There should only be minimal movement required for small group activities. Students should be seated if possible, every other seat, so that a teacher can sit in between to assist with behavior, and so that the students are not threatened by close proximity. This idea should be adapted with a mainstreamed class—the special student should feel safe and secure with the seating arrangement.

Classroom Management

Clearly and simply state your classroom rules so that each student knows what is to be expected of him or her. For example, in the Nassau Boces Elementary Program, where all students are multiply handicapped and in a special setting with small classes, there are three rules:

1. *Sit in your designated seat.*
2. *Ask before you touch.*
3. *Try your best.*

Each student will earn five checks each music class if they follow these rules. These rules are adapted to each individual's educational program (IEP) as part of a school-wide behavior management program. Each musical activity is evaluated and assessed according to the needs of the student. The points earned in music class are transferred to the classroom teacher's record for each student. Total points for the week earn privileges for each student as an important part of their growth recognition. The students have the power of choice and each choice has its positive or negative consequences.

Classroom Discipline

Event + Response = Outcome

Clearly state rules and consequences. Have students be role models for other students. Have leader's chair centrally located in the music classroom for all students to feel special when it is their turn to be the role model. Use cooperative learning techniques to foster positive interdependence between students. Use cooperative discipline techniques to foster a classroom with dynamics and mutual respect. A student will not become hostile or uncooperative if you make connections with acceptance, attention, appreciation, affirmation, and affection. In working with students with special needs, it is important to deal with the here and now, not yesterday. Reinforce the positive constantly. Direct nonthreatening suggestions for success. Know state/school regulations for the extreme and disruptive students.

Foundations of Music Education for Teaching Special Learners

A teaching attitude and approach that will serve the teacher of general, vocal, and instrumental music in today's diverse school populations. It is a multimodal technique that will ensure the successful inclusion and performance of students with specific learning disabilities; children from diverse backgrounds and cultures; those who are physically, mentally, psychologically, socially, and emotionally challenged; and at the opposite side of the spectrum, the talented and gifted.

Exceptional

Exceptional is a term used concurrently with the phrase "special learners" to define those children whose school performance shows significant discrepancy between ability and achievement and as a result require special instruction, assistance, and/or equipment.

IDEA
(Individual with Disabilities Education Act)

The IDEA was formerly called Public Law 94-142 or the Education for all Handicapped Children Act of 1975. It requires public schools to make available to all eligible children with disabilities a free appropriate public education in the least restrictive environment appropriate to their individual needs. Amendments were made to IDEA on June 4, 1997, to reauthorize and to make improvements.

IEP
(Individualized Education Program)

The IDEA requires public school systems to develop appropriate Individualized Education Programs (IEPs) for each child. The specific special education and related services outlined in each IEP reflect the individualized needs of each student. Music educators need to be sure that if a student is mainstreamed into the music program, all accommodations applicable to the program are met for successful inclusion. If not, consult your department chair, special education chair, and administrator for direction and assistance.

Related Services

Related services may include in-school individual counseling, in-school group counseling, speech/language therapy, physical and occupational therapy, art therapy, adaptive physical education, music therapy, itinerant services for the hearing impaired, itinerant services for visually impaired, and/or a sign language interpreter. These services are in addition to the child's academic special education program and would encompass the opportunity for the student to be included in the school's general music classes, and vocal and/or instrumental performance groups.

Public Law 504

If a suspected disability is not severe enough to warrant classification and services under IDEA, Public Law 504 provides an alternative to support related services or accommodations to benefit from an education. (May 2000, *A Guide to Disability Rights Laws,* U.S. Department of Justice Civil Rights Division, Disability Rights Section.)

CSE
(Committee on Special Education)

The CSE consists of a team of knowledgeable persons who decide what related services a child needs to receive that will support the academic special education process. The team generally includes the child's teacher; the parents or guardian; the child, if deemed appropriate; an agency representative who is qualified to provide or supervise the provision of special education; and other individuals at the parent's or agency's discretion. This multidisciplinary team is established in accordance with the provisions of section 4402 of the Education Law (State Education Department, *Vocational and Educational Services for Individuals with Disabilities*).

Due Process

Due process is the timeline that starts when you suspect a child may need special services. It is date- and time-specific, requiring a series of tests to be performed prior to the formalized CSE meeting. The due process is designed to protect the rights of parents of individuals with disabilities. The formal and informal procedures are for implementation, review and revision of an IEP.

Cognitive Functions

A term that pertains to thinking skills or mental processes.

Dysfunction

A term pertaining to the different functioning of the three phases of mental processing: input, elaboration, and output. The *input* phase is when the receiver takes in information. *Elaboration* is the process where the brain defines a task, comparing and integrating sources of information, planning, hypothesizing and working through problems logically, etc. The *output* phase is the skill of efficient communication that is accurate and appropriate. (Source: *Mediated Learning in and out of the Classroom,* 1996 Skylight Training and Publishing, Inc., Illinois.) Students with dysfunction in any of the three phases may be considered special learners and require adaptation in how information is presented.

Instructional Adaptations for Learning

Instructional adaptations for learning are carefully planned procedures tailored to each specific need that will help the student reach optimal learning. Instructional adaptations should be applied to students with behavior disorders, the mentally challenged, speech- and language-impaired, those with sensory deficits, physical and health disabilities, the ethnically diverse, and the gifted and talented. Each adaptation should make the student feel safe, secure, and successful in the music room.

Part 200 Regulations of the Commissioner of Education

Part 200 Regulations of the Commissioner of Education are issued from the New York State Education Department Office of Vocational and Educational Services for Individuals with Disabilities and serve to define the designating categories of students who have been identified as having a disability and who require special services and programs. The following thirteen designations and definitions are included in the Part 200.1 section of Regulations of the Commissioner of Education (pp. 12, 13, and 14) March 2000 document. This information is a public service and is essential for the music educator to know. The following designations and definitions are to be used by New York State teachers:

1. *Autism*—a developmental disability significantly affecting verbal and nonverbal communication and social interaction, generally evident before age three, that adversely affects a student's educational performance. Other characteristics often associated with autism are engagement in repetitive activities and stereotyped movements, resistance to environmental change or change in daily routines, and unusual responses to sensory experiences.

2. *Deafness*—a hearing impairment that is so severe that the student is impaired in processing linguistic information through hearing, with or without amplification, that adversely affects a student's educational performance.

3. *Deaf-blindness*—concomitant hearing and visual impairments, the combination of which causes such severe communication and other developmental and educational needs that they cannot be accommodated in special education programs solely for students with deafness or students with blindness.

4. *Emotionally disturbed*—a condition exhibiting one or more of the following characteristics over a long period of time and to a marked degree that adversely affects a student's educational performance:

(i) an inability to learn that cannot be explained by intellectual, sensory, or health factors;

(ii) an inability to build or maintain satisfactory interpersonal relationships with peers and teachers;

(iii) inappropriate types of behavior or feelings under normal circumstances;

(iv) a generally pervasive mood of unhappiness or depression; or

(v) a tendency to develop physical symptoms or fears associated with personal or school problems.

The term includes schizophrenia. The term does not apply to students who are socially maladjusted, unless it is determined that they have an emotional disturbance.

5. *Hearing impairment*—an impairment in hearing, whether permanent or fluctuating, that adversely affects the child's educational performance but that is not included under the definition of *deafness* in this section.

6. *Learning disability*—a disorder in one or more of the basic psychological processes involved in understanding or in using language, spoken or written, which manifests itself in an imperfect ability to listen, think, speak, read, write, spell, or to do mathematical calculations. The term includes such conditions as perceptual disabilities, brain injury, minimal brain dysfunction, dyslexia and developmental aphasia. The term does not include learning problems that are primarily the result of visual, hearing or motor

disabilities, of mental retardation, of emotional disturbance, or of environmental, cultural or economic disadvantage. A student who exhibits a discrepancy of fifty percent or more between expected achievement and actual achievement determined on an individual basis shall be deemed to have a learning disability.

7. *Mental retardation*—means significantly subaverage general intellectual functioning, existing concurrently with deficits in adaptive behavior and manifested during the developmental period, that adversely affects a student's educational performance.

8. *Multiple disabilities*—concomitant impairments (such as mental retardation-blindness, mental retardation-orthopedic impairment, etc.), the combination of which cause educational needs so that they cannot be accommodated in a special education program solely for one of the impairments. The term does not include deaf-blindness.

9. *Orthopedic impairment*—a severe orthopedic impairment that adversely affects a student's educational performance. the term includes impairments caused by congenital anomaly (e.g., clubfoot, absence of some member, etc.), impairments caused by disease (e.g. poliomyelitis, bone tuberculosis, etc.), and impairments from other causes (e.g., cerebral palsy, amputation, and fractures or burns which cause contractures).

10. *Other health-impairment*—having limited strength, vitality or alertness, including a heightened alertness to environmental stimuli, that results in limited alertness with respect to the educational environment, that is due to chronic or acute health problems, including but not limited to a heart condition, tuberculosis, rheumatic fever, nephritis, asthma, sickle cell anemia, hemophilia, epilepsy, lead poisoning, leukemia, diabetes, attention deficit disorder or attention deficit hyperactivity

disorder or Tourette syndrome, which adversely affects a student's educational performance.

11. *Speech or language impairment*—a communication disorder, such as stuttering, impaired articulation, a language impairment or a voice impairment, that adversely affects a student's educational performance.

12. *Traumatic brain injury*—an acquired injury to the brain caused by an external physical force or by certain medical conditions such as stroke, encephalitis, aneurysm, anoxia or brain tumors with resulting impairments that adversely affect educational performance. The term includes open or closed head injuries or brain injuries from certain medical conditions resulting in mild, moderate or severe impairments in one or more areas, including cognition, language, memory, attention, reasoning, abstract thinking, judgement, problem solving, sensory, perceptual and motor abilities, psychosocial behavior, physical functions, information processing, and speech. The term does not include injuries that are congenital or caused by birth trauma.

13. *Visual impairment including blindness*—an impairment in vision that, even with correction, adversely affects a student's educational performance. The term includes both partial sight and blindness.

Part 200 Regulations of the Commissioner of Education also include definitions of the different special education programs for which students with disabilities may be eligible. These programs could be a transitional support service or a structured learning environment that offers a twelve-month special program and implementation of each IEP. The complete Part 200 regulations can be downloaded from the VESID website: *www.nysed.gov/vesid*. For specific inclusion issues and for sites and phone numbers of VESID regional associates who interact with educators and parents, contact the VESID website or phone Cathy Castle at (518) 473-2878 for a listing.

Disorders Requiring Educational Interventions include:

1. Developmental Disorders; *Mental Disability.* Educable, Trainable, Severe, and Profound. The more severe the category the greater the possibility of associated features being present, such as seizures, visual, auditory, or cardiovascular problems. Other educational implications involve poor social skills, severe academic deficits, possible behavioral manifestations (i.e., low frustration tolerance, aggression, low self-esteem, and in some cases self-injurious behavior).

2. Pervasive Developmental Disorders; *Autistic Disorders.* The wide spectrum of serious developmental disorders that are characterized by severe impairment in the development of verbal and nonverbal communication skills, lack of social skills, and almost nonexistent imaginative activity. Asperger's syndrome, infantile autism, Fragile X, Kanner's syndrome, among other strains of autism have been identified by the scientific and medical community. With students with autism, educational implications include oppositional and aggressive behavior, seizures, low intellectual or very high intellectual development, poor social skills, and impaired cognitive functioning and language.

3. Specific Learning Disorders. *Mathematics Disorder* (Dyscalculia): serious marked disability in development of arithmetic skills that will require modifications like extended time, use of a calculator, revised test format. Poor self-esteem and social self-consciousness bring on avoidance and an increase of secondary problems. Dyscalculia often persists throughout the schooling years. It is not the result of mental retardation, inadequate teaching, or visual, hearing, or auditory deficits. *Disorder of Written Expression:* serious impairment in the ability to develop expressive writing skills. Also not the result of mental retardation, inadequate teaching, visual, hearing or

auditory deficits or neurological dysfunction. Some of the symptoms of this disorder are the inability to compose appropriate written texts, coupled with serious and consistent spelling errors, grammatical or punctuation errors and very poor organization of thought and text. As a means of covering up this problem, the student may exhibit a series of symptomatic behaviors, including avoidance, procrastination, denial, and possible disruptive behaviors when written assignments are given out. *Reading Disorders* (Dyslexia): Difficulty in decoding words and comprehension skills that significantly interfere in the child's academic performance. "As with most developmental disorders, this condition is not the result of mental retardation, inadequate educational experiences, visual or hearing defects, or neurological dysfunction" (p. 182, *Parent's Complete Special Education Guide,* The Center for Applied Research in Education, West Nyack, NY 1996, Dr. Roger Pierangelo and Mr. Robert Jacoby, authors). Other pervasive developmental disorders include *expressive language disorder, phonological disorder,* and *receptive language disorders.* Music teachers should be aware that according to Pierangelo and Jacoby, 3 to 10 percent of school-age children suffer from expressive language disorder, which may greatly hamper a child's social interaction skills as well as academic performance. The music room should be a people friendly place, a happy place, a place where abilities shine and deficits are destressed. What a student cannot say in language, he may say through music. Music is a language beyond words and transcends all educational systems and cultures.

4. Common disruptive behavior disorders are identified as *conduct disorders* and *oppositional defiant disorders.* Make sure each student in your music program knows the boundaries for his behaviors. Make sure rules are clearly stated and easy to follow. Make sure consequences to rules broken are as clearly stated and

faultlessly understood. Follow routine; address expectations of each activity or performance.

5. Common anxiety disorders of childhood are identified as *separation anxiety disorder, avoidant disorder* (child withdraws from social contact or interaction), and *overanxious disorder* (excessive level of anxiety or worry over a long period of time). For instance if a student shows withdrawal from being a leader of an activity or even volunteering where he has to pass out worksheets or instruments, etc., please tell him he will not fail and can feel safe. When he is ready he can volunteer for leadership. Otherwise, praise all participation activities to enhance self-esteem, self-worth, and security of child.

6. Physical disabilities are caused by many conditions. Some of the more common include: cerebral palsy—a condition characterized by poor muscle control spasticity; paralysis and other neurologic deficiencies resulting from brain injury that occurs during pregnancy, during birth, after birth or before age five. Four types of cerebral palsy are:

1. spastic,
2. choreoathetoid (muscles spontaneously move slowly without normal control),
3. ataxis (coordination is poor and movements are shaky), and
4. mixed (a combination or two or more types together).

Speech is difficult to understand in all forms of cerebral palsy, because the child has difficulty controlling the muscles involved in speech. Most children with cerebral palsy have other disabilities, such as below-normal intelligence; some have severe mental retardation. The *Merck Manual* reported that 40 percent of children with cerebral palsy have normal or above normal intelligence. About 25 percent with the spastic type have seizures (epilepsy). If you have a child with cerebral palsy in your music program, get specific instructions for signs of a seizure in your student and what to do when it happens. Above all, do not move the student. Report the seizure to the school nurse. immediately. (Definitions from *The Merck Manual of Medical Information,* complete and unabridged 1997 by PocketBooks of Simon & Schuster, NY.)

7. Limb deficiency. The condition of having a missing limb from birth or acquired after birth. The acquisition of an artificial limb (prosthesis) can be important to the physical and psychological well-being of the individual.

8. Muscular dystrophy is part of a group of inherited muscle disorders that lead to muscle weakness of varying severity. It is caused by a recessive gene and is carried on the X chromosome. It is a progressive disorder that eventually forces the child to become confined to a wheelchair. The different dystrophies, including Duchenne's and Becker's muscular dystrophies, differ in the expected life span of the child. Ninety percent of those with Becker's muscular dystrophy are still alive at the age of twenty, whereas those with Duchenne's are not.

9. Spina bifida is a condition in which one or more vertebrae fail to develop completely, leaving a portion of the spinal column unprotected. The risk of having a child with spina bifida is linked with having a deficiency of folate (folic acid) when pregnant. Many physical complications can occur from paralysis in areas below defect to hydrocephalus, bladder and kidney abnormalities, and physical deformities. Physical therapy keeps joints mobile and strengthens muscles.

10. Down syndrome is a chromosomal abnormality. A person normally has twenty-three pairs of chromo-

somes. In a person with Down syndrome, there is an extra chromosome, making three of a kind, called trisomy. Both physical and mental development is delayed. Children with Down syndrome can have a normal average IQ of 100, although many more have less in the 50 range. Physical characteristics (used to be called mongolism) are distinctive: a small head, broad face, flat slanting eyes and a short nose, large tongue, small low-set eyes, hands short and broad with a single crease across the palm. The pinkie often has only two sections instead of three and curves inward. They have a space between their first and second toes, but even with all of these characteristics they, like all children, have a tremendous capacity to appreciate music and the creative and performing arts. Their talents should be encouraged as it will be the key to their success in life.

11. Cystic fibrosis is a hereditary disease that causes certain glands to produce abnormal secretions, resulting in several symptoms, the most important of which affect the digestive tract and the lungs. It affects girls and boys equally. It develops from two abnormal genes that inhibit the transfer of chloride and sodium across cell membranes. When the transfer across cell membranes is disrupted, it leads to dehydration and stickiness of secretions. The glands are blocked and bacteria multiply. Gene therapy has held great promise for extending the life expectancy of a sufferer of cystic fibrosis. If a child is in your music program with cystic fibrosis and starts to cough or gag, please get medical attention immediately.

12. Infectious and communicable diseases in the schools. We have come a long way in curing once-incurable diseases, but today, there still are infectious diseases that school personnel, parents, and the community need to be aware of. They are chicken pox, cytomegalovirus (direct contact with blood or urine),

gonorrhea (bodily fluids, blood, or vaginal fluids), hepatitis A (fecal-oral), hepatitis B (direct contact with blood), herpes I (above waist), herpes II (below waist), HIV infection/AIDS, measles, mononucleosis (saliva), mumps (transmission through sneezing), respiratory syncytial virus (RSV) (nasal discharge), and *salmonella* bacteria (fecal-oral transmissions). (Source: p. 142, Pierangelo/Jacoby *Special Education Guide.* Center for Applied Research in Education, 1996.)

13. Visual impairments. The lack of vision or reduced vision may result in delays or limitations in motor, cognitive, and social development. If you have a blind or vision-impaired child in your music program, you may be quite surprised at the enhanced musical ability present. Without outside stimulus from the environment, the ear becomes keener. With music this is a plus and can provide a positive outlet and bridge for academic progress and performance. A high proportion of students with visual impairments have additional disabilities and may require a curriculum that includes reading and writing in Braille, listening skills, personal-social and daily living skills, orientation and mobility, career education, and instruction in the use of special aids and equipment. Read the child's IEP and make sure you make all necessary accommodations in the music room. Then delight in having a very important addition to your chorus or instrumental ensemble.

14. Hearing impairments may be a result from damage to the cochlea or the auditory nerve. This damage is caused by illness and disease (rubella, German measles, meningitis), RH incompatibility, hereditary factors, exposure to noise, and certain antibiotics. The child with a hearing impairment can gain great enjoyment from music class by being part of a group and experiencing sound through feeling vibrations, movement, and dancing and communicating through finger and hand signs. Just

like all children, there will be a large array of abilities among the hearing-impaired in your music program. If the IEP stipulates that your student has an sign interpreter for each class, make sure that covers the music class, too.

15. Eating Disorders are receiving special focus in the schools across the country. These too interfere with a student's ability to perform to the best of his/her ability. If you suspect anyone of your students is having difficulty in this area, bring this to the attention of the school psychologist, social worker or nurse personnel.

16. DisAbility Etiquette (John Cortez Jr. *On the Move*) August 2000.

    1. Ask Before You Help.

    2. Be Sensitive About Physical Contact.

    3. Think Before You Ask.

    4. Don't Make Assumptions.

    5. Respond Graciously to Requests.

Practice the Golden Rule: Do Unto Others As You Would Have Them Do Unto You.

ADA

(Americans with Disabilities Act)

The ADA prohibits discrimination on the basis of disability. An individual with a disability is defined in *A Guide to Disability Rights Law* (U.S. Department of Justice, May 2000) as a person who has a physical or mental impairment that substantially limits one or more major life activities, a person who has a history or record of such an impairment, or a person who is perceived by others as having such an impairment. The ADA does not specifically name all of the impairments that are covered. The ADA was enacted in July 1990. The private sector employment provisions are called Title I and became effective for employers with twenty-five or more employees on July 26, 1992, and on July 26, 1994 for employers of fifteen or more employees.

Title V of The Rehabilitation Act of 1973

This title of the law prohibits discrimination on the basis of a disability by the federal government, federal contractors, by recipients of federal financial assistance, and in federal programs and activities.

FAPE

(Free Appropriate Public Education)

Term used in P.L. 94-142 Individuals with Disabilities Act to mean special education and related services that are provided at public expense and conform to the state requirements and the individual's IEP.

Please make a note that the State Education Department in each state works hand in hand with the U.S. Department of Education in issuing regulations and requirements for the basic education of all children with and without disabilities, impairments, or handicapping conditions. For questions and issues in your music program, please contact the liaison to music and the performing arts in your State Education Department. In New York, contact Dr. Edward Marschilok, State Ed Department, Room 681 EBA, Albany, NY 12234, (Office) (518) 474-5932, *emarsch@mailnysed .gov* for Music Education, Curriculum, and Assessment.

TALENTED AND GIFTED

Have you ever had students who you knew could perform better than the results showed? These students so often experience boredom and frustration in school because they struggle to "fit in," but the reality is that they need to feel challenged by intellectual inquiry, exhilarated by discovery, full of bouncing vitality of gaining knowledge through creating, composing, inventing, hypothesizing, designing and synthesizing the world around them.

Section 902 of Public Law 95-561, the Gifted and Talented Children's Act of 1978, indicates that the term *gifted and talented* means children and, whenever applicable, youth who are identified at the preschool, elementary, or secondary level as possessing demonstrated or potential abilities that give evidence of high-performance capabilities in such areas as intellectual, creative, specific, or leadership ability or in the performing and visual arts. Their special abilities often require special attention and teaching techniques (U.S. Department of Education). Talented and gifted students are often distinguished by many of the following characteristics: advanced vocabulary for chronological age; outstanding memory; having lots of information, curious, asks "why?" and then "what next?"; has many interests, hobbies, and collections; may have a "passionate interest" that has lasted for many years; intense; gets totally absorbed in activities and thoughts; strongly motivated to do things that interest her; may be unwilling to work on other activities; may be reluctant to move from one subject area to another; operates on higher levels of thinking than his age peers; is comfortable with abstract thinking; perceives subtle cause-and-effect relationships; prefers complex and challenging tasks to "basic" work; may be able to "track" two or more things simultaneously (daydreaming and listening); catches on quickly, then resists doing work or works in a sloppy, careless manner; comes up with "better ways for doing things" and suggests them to peers, teachers, and other adults; sensitive to beauty and other people's feelings and emotions; advanced sense of justice and fairness; aware of global issues many age peers are uninterested in; sophisticated sense of humor; may be "class clown"; transfers concepts and learning to new situations; sees connections between apparently unconnected ideas and activities; may prefer the company of older children or adults; may prefer to work alone; resists cooperative learning; bossy in group situations; needs to constantly share all he knows; impatient when not called on to recite or respond; and may be "street smart" while not doing well on school tasks. (Source: *Teaching Gifted Kids in the Regular Classroom,* Susan Winebrenner, Free Spirit Publishing, 1992, p. 139 and 140).

The musical and the creative arts is an area where the talented and gifted can excel. Their creative thinking and perfectionist tendencies, directed by an understanding teacher/mentor, can enable that precocious student to develop wholesomely. All music lessons, classrooms, and performances are recommended to be geared to the six steps of Bloom's Taxonomy. Learning needs to follow a spiral-shaped curve that incorporates the following at each stage of developments. These concepts are listed from the bottom to the top of the spiral:

> 6. *Synthesis—Create*
> 5. *Evaluation—Judge*
> 4. *Analysis (Compare/Contrast)*
> 3. *Application*
> 2. *Comprehension*
> 1. *Knowledge*

This process was begun by each and every one of my university students to raise their disability awareness. After reporting on the disabilities, disorders, or impairments, each began stage 3 of "applying the knowledge" to the music classroom. Several class members worked this application through to include the highest skills of cognition, synthesis of class activities that would apply the knowledge in new and creative ways. Direct teaching—just the giving out of knowledge—does not give the student tools for lifelong learning. Applying, analyzing, evaluating, and creating engages the total person to use his or her gifts of multiple intelligence to find the ultimate power of expression for contribution to self, class, school, community, state, nation, and world.

Twice exceptional students are characterized by being talented and gifted and also having learning, perceptual, physical, or behavioral problems. While challenging the students, intellectually effective teaching practices for the disability, disorder, or impairment need to be applied along with constructive discipline practices. It is absolutely important to remember: If the student presents a danger to himself or to others, this needs to be brought to the attention of your direct supervisor, department chair, and administrators for further evaluation and action.

No matter what end of the spectrum your students are, their self-esteem has to be enhanced by the activities in the music program. Their feelings of self-worth need to be increased by recognition of the valuable contributions they make. For the special learner with low cognitive abilities and problems in processing, a teacher is absolutely necessary to guide the student outcomes. For a talented and gifted group, peer interaction and contribution will make class projects extraordinarily interesting. (See section on Teaching Critical Thinking Skills.)

ETHNICALLY DIVERSE STUDENTS

In addition to the talented and gifted student, the student with special learning disabilities, children from diverse backgrounds and cultures present a different type of challenge to the music teacher. These students may face at least two sets of expectations: those of their home and those of the school. They may not be fluent in the English language and may have communication difficulties of having English as a second language. We are fortunate as music educators because music is a universal language. A tremendously interesting curriculum can be devised for a music program using international music, customs, dances, and folklore to enrich all students in a multicultural perspective. We are all a part of the universe—Uni (One) Verse (Song). The following will serve as basic building blocks for development of teaching students from other cultures.

First and foremost besides understanding that we are all a part of one song is understanding universal emotions. Ed Young in *Voices of the Heart* (Scholastic Press, New York, 1997) invites all children young and old to explore the many voices from our hearts. The virtuous heart, the shameful heart, the understanding heart, the forgiving heart, the joyful heart, the sorrowful heart, the respectful heart, the rude heart, the contented heart, the despairing heart, the lazy heart, the able heart, the graceful heart, the forgetful heart, the resentful heart, the constant heart, the aspiring heart, the frightened heart, the merciful heart, the tolerant heart, the angry heart, the silenced heart, the evil heart, the doubtful heart, and the loyal heart. Mr. Young is an artist; he expresses his thoughts through Chinese characters and visual collage. As musicians we can teach these thoughts through the language of musical notation and sound. We can broaden the lives of our students by exposing them to pleasant sound experiences, starting with the magical sounds of nature. Tranquil ocean waves offer a sea of peace. Like the fetus in the womb, the protecting waters envelop and bring nourishment to the new life. There is a feeling of safety. Anger and aggression need not be displayed. The winds whistle, the brooks gurgle, the trees sigh, the horses neigh, the cats purr, the frogs croak, and the little lambs bleat. Quiet little musicians can be found in the tall summer grass waving in the breeze. There are fiddling crickets, buzzing bees, chattering squirrels, squealing mice, and trilling toads. All these are nice sounds, good sounds, pleasant to our ears. ("Loud, Louder, Loudest—Teaching the Dynamics of Life," E. S. Sobol, *New York State School Music News,* December 1998). Although the music one hears may be a little different, all ethnically diverse students have this common ground. All students have four basic needs to be met in music class and across the disciplines. This is described in *Stations of the Mind* (William Glasser, Harper & Row, 1982) and has developed into a theory for education called Choice Theory. A student will do well in school if he or she has a sense of:

1. *Belonging*

2. *Gaining power* (a student will grow in knowledge and skill and gain self-esteem through success. Through modeling a musical activity the student will gain power by successful mastery of same through realistic teacher direction)

3. *Having fun* (having fun improves health, builds positive relationships and enhances thinking. No matter how diverse the students are in the music classroom, activities need to have laughter. Students need to be uplifted and spirited to add to the quality of their successful program)

4. *Being free*—all students disturbed, challenged, or gifted, mainstreamed or not, need to express control of their own lives. They need to set goals, make plans, choose behaviors, evaluate results and learn from each experience to do things better (Sobol, *SMN,* December 1998).

In addition to filling the four basic above-mentioned needs in the music program for every student, the music educator should include music from past civilizations where for instance the universe was considered to be a world in tune with harmony. For the Chinese, music expressed a celestial order. For Indians, all things came from one sound, which entered both realms of the spiritual and the material. For the Greeks, music contributed to good health, curing illness of both the mind and body.

There are many sources on the market for learning more about multicultural education. Particularly helpful is the *Culture Catalog—Multimedia Resources in Folklore, History, Culture, and the Arts* for integration across the disciplines. It is published by City Lore: The New York Center for Urban Folk Culture, 72 East First Street, New York, NY 10003; phone (212) 529-1955; or find it online at *www.carts.org*. Another good source is *The World in Tune Catalogue,* Carousel Publications Ltd., Route 42, Sparrows Bush, New York, phone (212) 758-9399. *World in Tune* is an integrated approach to world music. Music was the center linked to all other disciplines. It is an approach geared to stimulate interest. Once an interest is aroused, the learning follows and all students are engaged in the process because they want to.

Diverse Populations of Gifted Children—Meeting Their Needs in the Regular Classroom and Beyond (Starr Cline and Diane Schwartz, published by Prentice-Hall, Inc. Simon & Schuster, New Jersey, 1999) is an up-to-date book filled with research on cultural and environmental factors that have shaped behaviors in specific populations. The authors cover characteristics of Asian Americans, African Americans, Native Americans, and Puerto Ricans. Each background may impact language, behavior and personal interactions, learning style, and values. Invite your students to share information about commonalities—festivals, flags, seasonal practices, and holidays. All can be united through music and the performing arts. Remember we live in one world. Let us share and learn from each other. Respect one another's dignity and be living proof and practice of the *Universal Declaration of Human Rights* (United Nations Publications, copyright 1989. *An Adaptation for Children* by Ruth Rocha and Otavio Roth, 1995).

There has been significant progress recently in discovering the mysterious and remarkable functions of the brain. However, "no computer has yet come close to matching the capabilities of the human brain" (*Merck Manual,* 1997 edition). Life is full of countless variations, including different learning styles. Musical/rhythmic intelligence is a language-related intelligence that goes beyond cultural bias and words themselves. Music and the creative cultural arts is an essential key to academic progress of all students, whether they have special needs, are talented and gifted, or are ethnically diverse. Music links our humanity to science, math, language arts, history, social studies, physical education, business, art, and drama. It is the center for our soul. Remember, the music room is to be a place where each and every student can feel safe, secure, and successful ("Music Success for Special Learners," E.S. Sobol, *School Music News,* March 1995).

Effective Teaching Strategies across the Disabilities

MENC (Music Educators National Conference) has identified in *Music for All Children* (1996 by VSA Educational Services, Distributed by Silver Burdett Ginn, NJ), a training program for music educators working with children with disabilities in regular education settings, four broad designations of disabilities. These designations are (1) Perceptual or Intellectual, (2) Speech and Language, (3) Behavioral, and (4) Orthopedic and other health impairments. For all categories of disabilities, it is recommended that the music educator:

- Maintain structure and routines in class.
- Give and reinforce instructions.
- Provide clear expectations for student performance in each activity.
- Give feedback immediately.
- Recognize appropriate behavior; address inappropriate behavior.
- Use the mood of the music to help pace the class.
- Model positive attitudes.

Effective teaching strategies need to be adapted for each category of disability. For children with perceptual or intellectual disabilities in addition, music educators should use the following effective teaching strategies:

- Using highly structured activities with clear expectations.
- Communicating in short sentences using a simple vocabulary.
- Pacing the class so that children are neither left behind nor bored.
- Providing immediate feedback, especially positive reinforcement.
- Recognizing appropriate behavior (provide immediate praise).

- Recognizing inappropriate behavior (provide immediate acknowledgment and constructive suggestions on appropriate behavior, establish rules and consequences to behavior).
- Modeling positive attitudes (be that which you want your student to emulate).

For children with behavioral disabilities, in addition music educators should:

- Maintain structure and standard routines in all aspects of the class.
- Consider ways to modify the environment to minimize distractions.
- Give specific and immediate feedback (positive reinforcement). Address inappropriate behavior immediately.
- Enlist the students in maintaining classroom decorum. (Source: *Music for All Children,* pp. 53, 75, 59)

For students with speech and language disabilities, in addition to those effective teaching strategies recommended by *Music for All Children,* use techniques to immediately assess their input, processing, and output. Use a microphone to build verbal responses. It in itself is an enhancement tool for the music classroom. Use of signing works as an effective tool to elicit and bridge verbal response and expression language arts.

For students with orthopedic or other health impairments, in addition to those effective teaching strategies already recommended, design lessons that will build reduced or limited strength, build motor skills, and enhance vitality by building self-esteem through music. Adapt chairs, desks, and musical instruments to reflect optimal learning conditions for student. Make sure the class matches requirements from student's IEP. If you do not have the proper modifications for the student, go to your immediate supervisor for direction and assistance to properly implement needs for the classroom environment. An effective music lesson has the following components:

- *Modeling:* Demonstrate a desired behavior before expecting students to perform the behavior.

- *Introducing new information in small steps:* Present the music activity by breaking it down into its components and then presenting the components one at a time.
- *Multimodal and multisensory presentation:* Single concept presented in variety of ways. Lessons should use audio-visual-tactile techniques for maximum student understanding.
- *Clues to facilitate recall:* Present new learning in ways that will assist the children in remembering the information. (Adapted from *Music for All Children,* p. 65)

Musical Process for Academic Progress

Introduction to Musical Literacy

To maximize learning for the student with special needs, concepts in music can be linked in a reality-based system that unites inside and outside of the classroom together to build applications for successful living for each study. For example, as an introduction to musical literacy, let us look first at the symbol of the universal stop light. The colors are red for stop, yellow for caution, and green for go. The world over, one will see this combination. Road signs are green; brake lights are red; yellow lines divide the lanes of traffic. As music teachers we can introduce these universal symbols to our students, building competence and confidence while developing a musical reading process. (Example 1, upside-down stoplight.) The *Green-Red* Song (Example 2) can be used to study high and low melodic pitches and the *Green, Yellow, Red Song* (Example 3) for adding a middle tone. Ear training can begin with three different-sized bongo drums or tom-toms. Work on drums can then be transferred to xylophone and keyboard for work in tonic, thirds, and fifths. Students at first will play the songs, responding aurally to teacher clues. Then the students will gradually combine ear and eye coordination to perform without teacher assistance. This lesson can be combined with a basic classroom management technique described in Daniel Goleman's book *Emotional Intelligence* (Bantam Books, New York 1995). The technique is called appropriately "The Stoplight Exercise." The components are:

Red Light:	1. Stop, calm down, and think before you act.
Yellow Light:	2. Say the problem and how you feel.
	3. Set a positive goal.
	4. Think of lots of solutions.
	5. Think ahead to the consequences.
Green Light:	6. Go ahead and try the best plan.

The stoplight notion offers a concrete set of steps for dealing with those momentous moments in the classroom. Beyond the management of feelings, it points a way to a more effective action. As a way of handling the unruly emotional impulse of thinking before acting, it becomes a basic technique for dealing with situations with school-aged children.

Upside Down Stop Light

Example 1

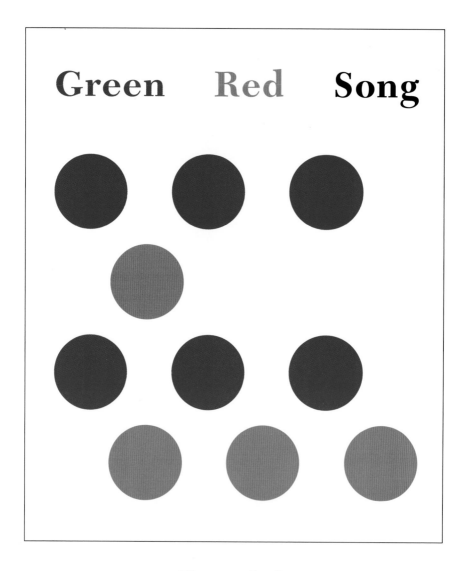

Example 2

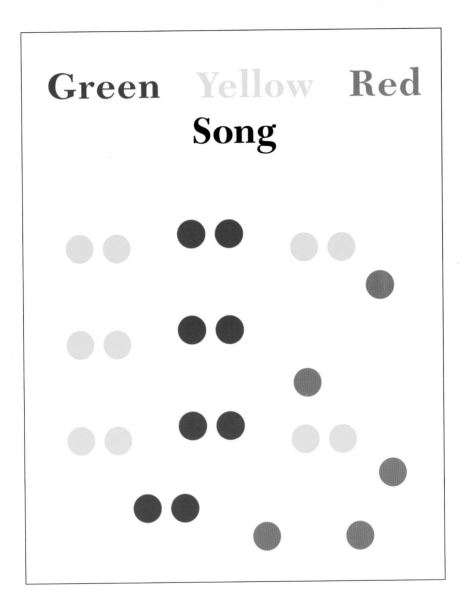

Example 3

Class Structure—
Sound Signals

On the open seas, sound and light signals are used to communicate directions. All military personnel understand these signals for navigation. Applying this principle to the music class: From the first introduction to red as the low tone and green as the high tone, the music teacher can establish directions for classroom management. (Example 4) These signals are based on the way we speak.

Please stand up:
low, low, high = red, red, green.

Please sit down:
high, high, low = green, green, red.

Adding our middle tone, yellow color, we say,
Please get in line:
high, high, middle, low = green, green, yellow, red.

Bring closure to class by saying,
Good job:
high, low = green, red.

Sound Signals for Classroom Management

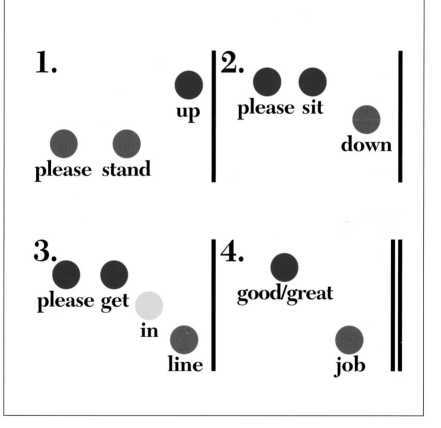

1.

up

please stand

2.

please sit

down

3.

please get in

line

4.

good/great

job

Example 4

Sound Signals to Melodic Understanding

Active music listening helps special learners build their ability to focus and build concentration. Letters are to syllables as dots are to musical notes. Prereading skills of following the rhythmic impulse of words in a song can be combined with ear training for steps and skips in a scale as well as numerical drills. (Examples 5a, b, and c)

Depending on the level of the students, link to the language arts, math, science, social studies, physical and health education, drama, art, business and technology curriculums through creative melodic drills. Identify the seven letters of the musical alphabet with number dot cards. Transfer the concept of the seven letters of the musical alphabet to seven days of the week, seven wonders of the world, seven colors of the rainbow, seven tones of the diatonic scale, seven chakras or energy systems in our body, seven dwarfs in *Snow White,* and so on.

Prereading Skills Link through Melodic Drills

Letters/Syllables   Dots/Musical Notes

Example 5

Sound Signals to Melodic Understanding

Letters/Syllables = Dots/Musical Notes

● ●
Sunday

● ●
Monday

● ●
Tuesday

● ●
Wednesday

● ●
Thursday

● ●
Friday

● ● ●
Saturday

Example 5a

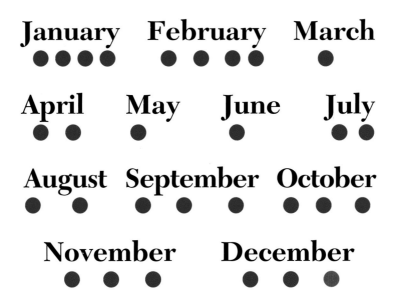

Example 5b

How Many Syllables
(sounds)

How Many Notes?
(dots)

June

July

September

January

Continue
concept with
all 12
months

Example 5c

Introduction to
Rhythmic Notation

(Examples 6a, b, and c) The rhythm of a song is the heartbeat of the music. For special learners this can first be described by doing a motor activity: Stop (Whole Note), Stand Up (Half Note), Walk (Quarter Notes), Jog (Eighth Notes), Run (Sixteenth Notes). A description can follow of a simple story like this . . . In the Beginning there was only One sound. All sounds lived in this One sound. There was so much sound in the One sound that the Whole note had to divide. When a whole note divides it grows a stem. When a half note divides it gets colored in. When a quarter note divides it grows a flag. Two flags join together with a beam, and so forth. Rhythm drills consistently use green and red notes, this time to signify fast and slow rhythms. Link song syllables to rhythmic impulse in learning choral works and identification of repertoire in games such as "Name That Tune." Demonstrate a train moving from slow to high speed through correlation of rhythm. Speak about formation that birds have in the sky, marching bands on the football field, etc.

Introduction to Rhythm

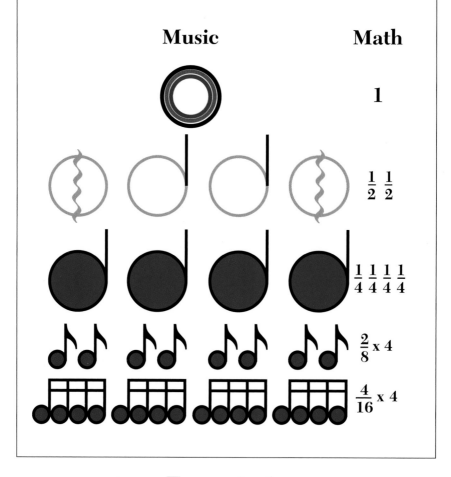

Example 6a

Rhythm Drills

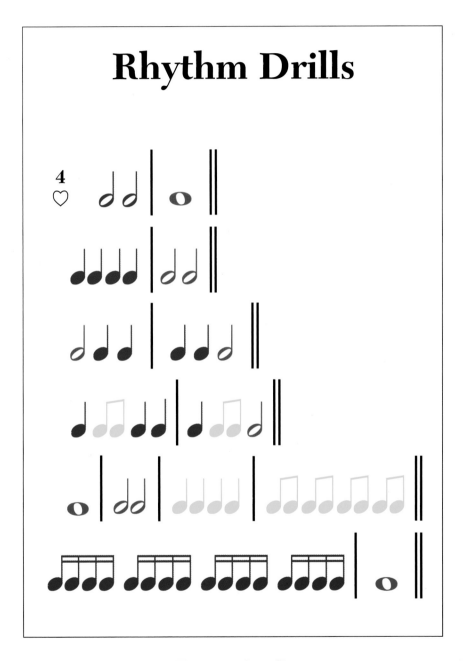

Example 6b

Name That Tune

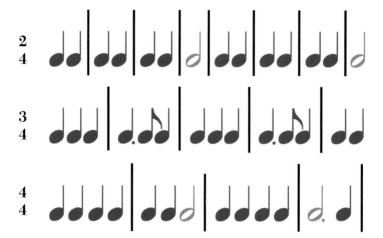

²⁄₄ **Twinkle, Twinkle, Little Star**

³⁄₄ **My Country 'Tis of Thee**

⁴⁄₄ **Old MacDonald Had a Farm**

Example 6c

Reading Notation on a Staff

Using Example 7a, b, and c, students are instructed to either fold or draw lines connecting the two horizontal dots so that we get a picture that has five lines and four spaces. (Link math—distance between two points is a line.) Place dots (reading from left to right) from bottom to top (feet to head), first line, first space; second line, second space; third line, third space; fourth line, fourth space; fifth line, fifth space. Arrange dots in an ascending line. Show manual staff by pointing out how to count the lines and spaces on one's hand. Ask for simple addition of five plus four equaling nine. Then link musical theory of inversion of intervals with the nine planets of our solar system and their lines of orbit and the harmony of ternary triads. Nine symbolizes our three worlds—body, intellect, and soul. It symbolizes eternity completion and incorruptibility. It is a number sacred in Christianity. In Judaism, it is the number of truth. *Jiu* (nine) is the number of eternity in Chinese tradition and a celestial number whose importance outshines all others. Indian mandalas are based on multiplications of nine symbolizing the universe. Our solar system is made up of these nine known planets: from nearest to the sun Mercury, Venus, Earth, Mars, Jupiter, Saturn, Uranus, Neptune, and Pluto. The ancients believed that the universe was considered to be a world in tune with harmony. For the Indian, all things come from one sound entering both realms of the spiritual and the material. For the Greeks, music contributed to good health, curing illnesses of both mind and body. Review in the beginning, there was a whole note. The world was one. All sounds were one. (Introduction to musical literacy came full circle.)

Reading Notation on a Staff

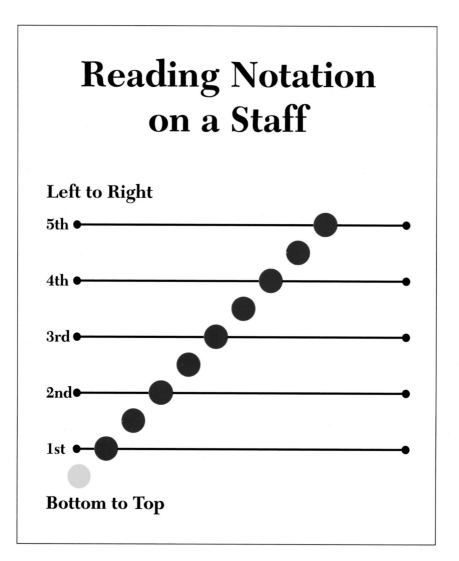

Example 7a

Uni-verse
One Song #9

Example 7b

In the beginning there was One Sound

Applications to Choral and Instrumental Programs

Literature for both choral and instrumental performance ensembles should be carefully chosen for special learners to gain self-esteem and competence. The work should have a universal and global message in its expression of emotion, demonstration of contrasts, and overall form of characterization and dramatization. While studying world music literature we want to embrace the cultural diversity of the new Americans. At the same time we also want to celebrate aspects of American culture through our own music by studying Native American music and great American composers, including Scott Joplin, Stephen Foster, Leonard Bernstein, Aaron Copland, Walter Piston, Karel Husa, Alan Hovhaness, and John Philip Sousa, to name a few. Alternate special ensembles for choral literature and alternate special ensembles for instrumentalists, for example with choir chimes, steel drums, and ethnic instruments. This can be the draw to maintain interest, develop confidence, and build socialization skills for all learners.

Success for Students of All Challenges and Learning Styles

When the special music educator can present his musical concepts in a multisensory mode that combines **auditory**, **tactile**, and **visual** feedback, he or she will reach learners of all capabilities. The musical/rhythmic intelligence activates whole brain learning. It serves to link our humanity to science, math, language arts, history, social studies, physical education, business, art, dance, drama and theater, building a bridge for success to students of all challenges and learning styles.

The National and
State Standards for
Learning in the Arts

National Standards for Learning in the Arts

There are nine national standards for music education and learning in the arts.

1. Singing, alone and with others, a varied repertoire of music.
2. Performing on instruments, alone and with others, a varied repertoire of music.
3. Improvising melodies, variations, and accompaniments.
4. Composing and arranging music within specified guidelines.
5. Reading and notating music.
6. Listening to, analyzing, and describing music.
7. Evaluating music and music performances.
8. Understanding relationships between music, the other arts, and disciplines outside the arts.
9. Understanding music in relation to history and culture.

The New York State Education Department urges all teachers in the state to use learning experiences of highest value for the development of their students. Lessons should engage students' interest and press them toward growth and learning. Lessons should be easily adaptable to other classroom and/or clearly adaptable to many different kinds of students. Lessons should have values beyond the classroom.

The nine national standards are consolidated to four New York State Standards for Learning in the Arts as follows:

1. Creating, performing, and participating in the arts.
2. Knowing and using arts materials and resources.
3. Responding to and analyzing works of arts.
4. Understanding the cultural dimensions and contributions of the arts.

Criteria for assessment and evaluation have been given by the New York State Education Department for students with and without severe disabilities. Teachers should contact NYSED for proper assessment practices and coordinate efforts with their school district. The integration of whole language activities in the music classroom and mediated learning experiences in the special education and inclusion classroom are two approaches that enable the music teacher to reach the standards for all students in their programs.

Whole Language Activities through Music

In teaching music to special learners, whole language activities through music of listening, speaking (singing), reading (notation), and writing (composing) creatively touch all four standards with even the simplest of themes.

Whole language is four-pronged. It encompasses listening, speaking, reading, and writing. These four elements are found in music. A music student can:

1. Increase his attention span through guided listening experiences.

2. Speak through vocal and instrumental expression.

3. Develop reading ability through graphic representation of sounds through music notation, traditional and otherwise.

4. Develop creative writing abilities by making up adapted songs, putting songs to stories, and organizing curriculum concepts in rhythm and rhyme.

There are many assets to this program:

1. The student's day is more integrated from class to class through organizing themes.

2. Students are empowered to take responsibility for their own education.

3. Learning is student centered.

4. Teachers are life-long learners giving vibrancy to every single exchange.

5. Teachers impact joy through their work allowing students to excel to the best of their potential.

6. Music becomes life itself, instruction to the mind as well as the heart.

Letters/Syllables
as
Dots/Musical Notes

•••• •••••••• •••• ••••••••

••• ••• ••• ••• •• •• • •

Letters make words like "Go" and "Stop".

Dots make notes that *Beat* like a *clock*.

Syllables form words to make good sense.

Notes form rhythms which sound an event.

Whole Language Activity

- Whole note divides into two half notes.
- Two half notes divide into four quarter notes.
- Four quarter notes divide into eight eighth notes.
- Eight eighth notes divide into sixteen sixteenth notes.

- A Half Note is a Whole Note with a Stem.
- A Quarter Note is a Half Note Colored In.
- Eighth Notes wave a flag out from the Stem.
- Two flags mean Sixteenth Notes faster then.
- Beams connect a single or double flag.
- Dot after a note adds plus one.

Mediated Learning in the Special Education and Inclusion Classroom

It was with great anticipation that I got clearance from Nassau Boces for me to take a course in Mediated Learning in the Special Education and Inclusion Classroom. During the summer of 1999 when I spoke about teaching music to special learners at the ABI/IBC 26th International Congress on Arts and Communications at the Ritz Four Seasons Hotel in Lisbon, Portugal, I was approached by the renowned Israeli conductor Dahlia Atlas who felt I should meet Dr. Reuven Feuerstein, the founder and director of the International Center for Enhancement of Learning Potential in Jerusalem. Professor Atlas felt that I was practicing MLE in the music classroom and that I could learn a great deal from Dr. Feuerstein, and that my work in the music classroom would be of interest to him. Dr. Feuerstein and I are presently in correspondence and a trip will be arranged in the near future for me to bring my ideas of using MLE in the music classroom to his work.

Mediated learning is a process by which the teacher helps his student get the desired result. This technique is instrumental for enhancing the learning potential of every severely challenged student in the Nassau Boces Elementary Program at Jerusalem Avenue, North Bellmore, Long Island. The approach of MLE is demonstrated in an action plan for William as well as a detailed six-week lesson plan for using mediated learning techniques to enhance musical literacy as well as ear training. Mediated learning techniques are used while addressing New York State Standards for Students with Severe Disabilities.

Action Plan

I am delighted to report that from the onset of the Mediated Learning class with Ms. Randi Azar, my classes benefited from the mediation process on multi-levels.

As a result of the techniques used all 176 students were able to improve their cognitive responses in the music classroom. Their behaviors improved consistently since I immersed myself in becoming proficient in the methods and materials of mediated learning.

Each of my 24 special education classes have three rules for the music classroom. Rule Number 1 is: Sit in the designated seat. Rule Number 2 is: Ask before you touch. Rule Number 3 is: Try your best. All classes have students with severe social, emotional, psychological and/or learning disabilities. I found that with more mediation, fewer problems occurred when the classes made a transition to the music room. By putting a red dot on the designated seat, there seemed almost no error when the students would enter my room. Without the dot it seemed day after day, the students would get out of their line order, get confused over who was first, second, third, etc. Valuable time was lost getting each class seated. With the red dot posted outside on my rule sheet and the red dot on the back of the chair, the students had a simple guide and they were able to achieve success in getting seated at the beginning of class. Since many of the students suffer from complications of ADHD, their hands often do touch without permission and there are discipline problems. Further reinforcement of proper behavior regarding playing musical instruments during an activity helped achieve intentionality and reciprocity. Holding the students responsible for understanding their activities enabled them to try their best. Encouraging their own thinking kept their interest, kept their challenge and made them quite proud of their achievements no matter how large or small.

One particular eight-year-old boy whose name is William showed some remarkable improvements in the music classroom over the past five weeks of the NYSUT class.

William has severe behavioral problems. He is oppositional. He gives threats of violence. He has poor concentration. He has low frustration tolerance. He is impulsive. He is easily distracted. He is quite moody. He has poor social skills. He has perceptual motor deficits. He has moderate to severe attention deficit problems and has shown suicidal tendencies. When faced with work that he feels is too difficult he becomes angry and verbally abusive. All this aside, he has shown (for the three years I have had him as a music student) interest in every music class. He has a smile which lights up the room and a strong rhythmic sense that has helped other students excel. I have built his strengths upon strengths and he has delighted in learning. I was thrilled when he could play the red, green songs and even more thrilled when he led the class in following the musical dots of the *Nutcracker March*. Not only did he show hand-eye coordination, he was able to highlight the musical movement on the page by choosing the bright yellow marker. After he highlighted the notes on the page, he could then play it on the keyboard transferring up and down, steps, skips, and repeated notes with directionality on the keyboard. Another area of excellence was shown in ear training. He was able to comprehend the story of the *Nutcracker* and recognize seven tunes from the ballet. This for a normally functioning eight-year-old student is a good achievement; for William and his peers, it was extraordinarily exciting.

Sample Lessons: Lesson No. 1

- Target Skill: High and Low in Sound and Space
- Age Range: Special Education Students ungraded age 5–10 adapted to 24 different classes with different disabilities
- Time Range: General Music Class meeting twice a week for 30 min.
- Mediated Learning Techniques Used While Addressing NYS Standards The Four New York State Standards for Students with Severe Disabilities

1. Creating, Performing, and Participating in the Arts
Intentionality and Reciprocity
Students will be introduced to high and low pitch through size analysis of instruments. Students will conclude through creative discovery that the large size instrument has the lower pitch and that the smaller instrument has the higher pitch. The mediator will help guide the students' ability to categorize similar instruments by size and draw specific and general conclusions about sound.

2. Knowing and Using the Arts
Meaning
The mediator will direct students to understand that this musical concept is scientifically based. Experiments with instruments found in nature and instruments created by humans will be conducted, i.e., flower pots, seed pods, eggs, coffee cans, rubber bands, unpitched rhythm instruments, pitched instruments, string families, woodwind families, brass families, percussion families.

3. Responding to and Analyzing Works of Art
Transcendence
This first lesson opens up to the students a new way of seeing that is critical to understanding cultural dimensions in the arts. The students will apply the multisensory style of seeing, touching, and feeling to each new challenge. They will begin to understand specific voice ranges of instruments based on the size of the instruments. They will begin to understand written notation and the placement of notes on the staff for high and low pitches (directionality). By looking at a drum set they would know the

order of the different drums and cymbals with application of the size/sound concept. Socially, the students will begin to hear differences in their sound environments. Emotionally, the students will expand their understanding of stimulus and reactions within their world. High and low will become important tools in their cognitive growth.

4. Understanding the Cultural Dimensions and Contributions of the Arts

Competence, Sharing, Individuation, Goal-Setting, and Challenge

With knowledge, students can feel competence. This lesson fosters competence, sharing, and individuation. The long-term goal is to enhance listening skills through music activities and bridge the ability to focus in other subject areas.

As music education lessons progress and the students start to learn to create melodies from different sounds and harmonies from stacking sounds, students will be repeatedly challenged to discover sound where he or she would not have listened before.

• Lesson Assessment Using Alternate Performance Indicators for Students with Severe Disabilities + = Frequently, / = Evident, o = Developing

• All students will be assessed three ways. Teacher will direct response through class demonstration. Teacher will play Side 1 of *Ear Training For Children* (E. S. Sobol) and assess individual students' responses to questions of high and low sounds on tape. Third, student will follow color code of red for low and green for high and perform simple high low songs on tone bells, maracas, and hand drums. Student responses will be kept in individual class folders.

Self-change—This primary lesson of discovering that the smaller instrument has the higher pitch and the larger instrument has the lower pitch has brought safety, security, and success to each student. This self-change is assessment and will serve the student as one tool for problem solving in different situations. "Do you hear what I hear?" "How do you know it is what you say?" "Shake it, strike it, pluck it—what has the higher pitch and why?" "How do you know that that is a train whistle and not a fire engine signal?"

Sample Lessons: Lesson 2

- Target Skill: Same Sound/Different Sound
- Age Range: Special Education Students ungraded age 5–10 adapted to 24 different classes with different disabilities
- Time Range: Part of six-week plan, general music class meeting twice a week for 30 minutes.
- Mediated Learning Techniques Used While Addressing the NYS Standards for Students with Severe Disabilities.

1. Creating, Performing, and Participating in the Arts
Intentionality and Reciprocity
Students will differentiate between same two-note pattern with different two-note patterns on the same instrument. Students will differentiate between same two-note pattern with different two-note patterns on instruments of different timbres (piano, violin, bell, drum, and guitar). This lesson is bridged to teaching about directionality in music. Students will learn to differentiate sounds going up (ascending) and going down (descending).

2. Knowing and Using the Arts
Meaning
The mediator will help build the students' vocabulary in the sound environment. Same sound and different will be spoken, sung, and played. This is a very important beginning of a life-long concept in music education for musical literacy as well as in adaptive daily living.

3. Responding to and Analyzing Works of Art
Transcendence
When in music, art, dance, or theater, *same* and *different* are paramount and fundamental for building success. Throughout history comparisons connect people around the world. Signals on the open seas are universal by sound. Sound creates meaning and meaning creates communication.

4. Understanding the Cultural Dimensions and Contributions of the Arts
Competence, Sharing, Individuation, Goal-setting, Challenge, and Self-Change

The ear training activities form a basis for all students to focus and distinguish. It bridges their language arts, sciences, social studies, math and physical education. Same note and different note are premusic-reading skills. These bridge to letters, numbers, and signs. At this stage of development in the music class. I have used this lesson to introduce a structure for my class discipline. "Please sit down" is translated into music pitches on high, high, low, 5-5-1. "Please stand up" is low, low, high, 1-1-5. "Please get in line," 5-3-2-1, high, middle, step, down. And this lesson begins to form concepts of melody and harmony, concepts universal throughout the world, while establishing order in the classroom.

- Lesson Assessment— + = Frequently, / = Evident,
            o = Developing

- Students will be assessed on same and different by *Ear Training for Children* (Side 2). They will write S for same and D for different on worksheet. Second they will play color-coded simple melodies with red and green for same, different, high, and low. They will create their own same different songs and have their peers perform them in class with the student composer as conductor.

- This lesson builds on the student's success from Lesson 1 and adds to their competence and self-esteem. Student work will be kept in their class folder and behavior kept on index cards arranged by class.

Sample Lessons: Lesson 3

• Target Skill: Rhythm in Sound

• Age Range: Special Education Students ungraded age 5–10 adapted to 24 different classes with different disabilities.

• Time Range: Third part of six-week plan, general music class meeting twice a week for 30 minutes.

• Mediated Learning Techniques Used While Addressing the NYS Standards for Students with Severe Disabilities.

1. Creating, Performing, and Participating in the Arts

Intentionality and Reciprocity

This lesson reveals to the students that all things living have a rhythm. Play, hear, and feel your heartbeat. What is your name? Is it Bill?—one sound. Is it Mary?—two sounds. Is it Patricia?—three sounds. This is next in the series of ear training activities. From first names to last names to full names, students can show their listening skills by playing on rhythm instruments, singing, and notating the rhythm. This lesson is bridged to teaching about tempos in rhythm.

2. Knowing and Using the Arts

Meaning

From identifying one, two, three or four-beat rhythms, students can extend their vocabulary and sound banks by starting to hear accents or stressed sounds in contrast to unaccented on nonstressed sounds. Whatever the classroom lesson in this music can correlate its content. Study of fruit—a student can categorize the fruits by sound. Pear—one sound; apple—two sounds; pineapple—three; watermelon—four sounds. These sounds will then be turned into musical symbols, necessary prereading skills.

3. Responding to and Analyzing Works of Art

Transcendence

The students in the Nassau Boces Elementary Program are all below grade level, having tracking problems in math and reading. This performance activity enables each student with the instrument of their choice—drum set, hand drums, maracas, or bells—to perform a small story in sound. They can play the rhythm of the song and then perform the rhythm of the words of the song. These are two different activities that go hand in hand and transcend to their ability to process what they bear and improve their overall school performance.

4. Understanding the Cultural Dimensions and Contributions of the Arts

Competence, Sharing, Individuation, Goal-Setting, Challenge, and Self-Change

Universally, a person's competence grows with familiarity. This lesson is a beginning activity in growing familiar with the sounds around, acoustic natural sounds and sounds of civilization. The sounds have an order. This order forms the basis for language development and is heard in melodies. Rain, ocean, summer nights, waterfalls, giggling, and crying are just a few of the sounds that have a rhythm and a pattern that become identifying characteristics. For this activity and the sophistication of the students, rhythms of sound were confined to the language arts program and its vocabulary of words, which students should know by the time they leave the program. Through group class projects, the students perform their compositions clearly identifying rhythm—in music, speech, and language while at the same time teachers can broaden their students' sound environments by assessment activities such as the one listed below.

• Lesson Assessment— + = Frequently, / = Evident,
o = Developing

• Through echo-response activities all students will be assessed on their improved abilities to differentiate sounds and syllables. This will serve to improve their aural processing and help them throughout their education in listening, following directions, and auditory processing.

Sample Lessons: Lesson 4

- Target Skills: Reading notes on a musical staff
- Age Range: Special Education Students ungraded age 5–10 adapted to 24 different classes with different disabilities
- Time Range: Fourth part of six-week plan, general music class meeting twice a week for 30 minutes.
- Mediated Learning Techniques Used While Addressing the NYS Standards for Students with Severe Disabilities.

1. Creating, Performing and Participating in the Arts
Intentionality and Reciprocity
This lesson introduces lines and spaces which comprise the musical staff on which a clef is placed to denote the name of each line and space. Correlation of lines and spaces is shown on one's hand—the fingers the five lines and in between the lines are the spaces. Students are guided through drills to identify a note on a line or in a space. After which students are shown the G clef, which names the second line of the staff as G (treble clef) following the musical alphabet of A, B, C, D, E, F, G, up the staff (going higher) and down the staff (going lower) . Lessons 1, 2, and 3 are reviewed so that the students can clearly understand on writing what it is they heard in sound. Other clefs are introduced briefly—the F clef, which is for bass clef, and the various C clefs, which name middle C where the clef is placed.

2. Knowing and Using the Arts
Meaning
Musical literacy is a wonderful way of giving confidence to a special learner. Is the note on a line? Is it in a space? Does the melody go by steps, or skips? The reading skills are rooted not in a rhyme but in the placement of the clef. Playing the notes on a keyboard helps with reading skills because the notes become visual as they ascend or descend. Adding right hand and left hand helps both sides of the brain develop as eye and hand coordination is added to cognitive development.

3. Responding to and Analyzing Works of Art
Transcendence

Musical Notation is a sign for sound. Just as the written word gives freedom of expression to the writer, so to the notated note gives freedom of expression to the composer. It is this element besides the element of interpreting others' ideas, that is so exciting to the special learner. His or her abilities can shine in composition—the structure of the language is not as complicated as that of English. The musical alphabet is limited to seven letters, not twenty-six or more. The staff has five lines with ledger lines, which can be added to make the sounds extend higher or lower. Just like reading books, reading musical notation gives the performer the freedom to discover music from all cultures, and periods of history.

4. Understanding the Cultural Dimensions and Contributions of the Arts

Competence, Sharing, Individuation, Goal-Setting, Challenge, and Self-Change

Although the students I teach are just beginners in learning how to read a note on a musical scale, they delight in games of putting words together from the musical alphabet and figuring out how to write them on the musical staff on the blackboard. They feel good as they gain confidence in writing the notes and the corresponding English letters that identify both worlds to them, language and music. They share in compiling name lists, they set goals to see how many words they can think of. They are challenged because their spelling vocabulary is just starting and they are able to assess not only their own development in the music activity but their classroom behavior during the music class. Writing, reading, and speaking/composing, reading, and performing enhance the individuation of each learning experience to the benefit of each class.

• Lesson Assessment— + = Frequently, / = Evident,
o = Developing

• All students will complete worksheets that will show the teacher whether they can name the lines and spaces in the treble clef. The worksheets will show their understanding of high and low notes on the treble clef and their placement on the piano keyboard. Students will compose a simple four-bar melody on the treble clef staff with the assistance of the teacher.

Sample Lessons: Lesson 5

- Target skills: Finding Patterns in Music
- Age Range: Special education students ungraded age 5–10 adapted to 24 different classes with different disabilities
- Time Range: Fifth part of six-week plan, general music class meeting twice a week for 30 minutes
- Mediated Learning Techniques Used While Addressing the NYS Standards for Students with Severe Disabilities.

1. Creating, Performing, and Participating in the Arts
Intentionality and Reciprocity
Through reviewing familiar songs that the students know well, students identified by ear and body percussion, by letter and pencil and paper, and echo and response two patterns. One pattern was with a song starting with the chorus first, then the verse, i.e., "Tingaleyo"; the second pattern was with the verse first, i.e., "Eye of the Tiger"; then the chorus. Eight different songs were categorized with the intention to move ahead and teach the *March of the Nutcracker Suite,* their first song of the year that had no words.

2. Knowing and Using the Arts
Meaning
Lesson 5 uses skills learned in all previous lessons. What is the meaning of a pattern? Where do you find patterns? How does a pattern help with the structure or architecture of a piece of music. Can you tell the form of a piece knowing its pattern?

3. Responding to and Analyzing Works of Art
Transcendence
Guided listening experiences offer the best mediation possible for learning the different styles of music as well as learning the patterns of each individual piece, be it a simple song, a sonata, fantasia, or fugue. The identification of the components make for a greater understanding. With greater understanding, mastering a composition becomes an exciting adventure. It is like having a tour guide give a minute-by-minute commentary on the sights that you are seeing.

4. Understanding the Cultural Dimensions and Contributions of the Arts

Competence, Sharing, Individuation, Goal-Setting, Challenge, and Self-Change

From a song to a ballet, from words to a story without words, from sneakers to toe shoes, the six-week plan of lessons was geared to open the door of opportunity for the special education students to see a professional ballet company perform a traditional ballet, *The Nutcracker* by Tchaikovsky. The goals were to have these severely disabled students control their behavior for an hour in a large auditorium filled with the entire school, students and staff and also follow the story, keeping focused for an hour. Starting with the patterns for familiar songs to the new music of the *March of the Nutcracker* was a start. Every time they heard the music, since the experience was guided by hand clapping and patting activities, reading the notes, playing the notes, the students' interest was engaged. A video of the ballet was shown prior to the dance company coming. In this technology-oriented society, students are used to watching a screen and not interacting. This helped them prepare for the live version of the *Nutcracker.* Mediating through a multisensory style of teaching reached all students. The outcome of the live performance raised the standard of task focus by 99 percent. The ballet was a true successful experience.

• Lesson Assessment— + = Frequently, / = Evident,
o = Developing

• All students will show me without teacher direction and through body percussion the pattern of eight familiar songs. Clapping will be for the theme or chorus of the song and patting will be for the verse of the song. Teacher then will play a song completely unfamiliar to the students, and they will have to discover through repeated listening what the pattern of the song will be. Teacher will model the response for the low-level classes. Middle and higher-level classes will discover the pattern through guided questions of what to listen for.

Sample Lessons: Lesson 6

- Target Skills: Name the Tune in *Nutcracker*
- Age Range: Special education students ungraded age 5–10 adapted to 24 different classes with different disabilities
- Time Range: Sixth part of six-week plan, general music class meeting twice a week for 30 minutes
- Mediated Learning Techniques Used While Addressing the NYS Standards for Students with Severe Disabilities

1. Creating, Performing, and Participating in the Arts

Intentionality and Reciprocity

As a follow-up activity for seeing the *Nutcracker Ballet* all students will see if they can recognize at least five out of seven of the tunes from the *Nutcracker.* The tunes presented were (1) March, (2) Arab Dance, (3) Chinese Dance, (4) Dance of the Reed Flutes, (5) Russian Dance, (6) Dance of the Sugar Plum Fairy, and (7) Waltz of the Flowers. The process is teacher-directed for the name of the melodies as well as the spelling of the titles as the students find the letters they recognize. All tunes recognized are a great achievement for these special learners. Two out of seven, one out of seven, three out of seven, all is a stretch for the kids and an exciting result of MLE.

2. Knowing and Using the Arts

Meaning

Each dance was given a visual image for the students to connect with. Each dance was compared in pattern and character. Each dance was played repeatedly with the name to prepare students to take the plunge and guess the name of the tune on their own, without assistance.

3. Responding to and Analyzing Works of Art

Transcendence

Learning seven tunes from the ballet and seeing how the costumes fit the movement of the dance and how the scenery changed with the story all enlightened the students. It also awakened them to an area of beauty that some would never have experienced. Other great works of music literature can be presented to the students now that this presentation was such a great success.

4. Understanding the Cultural Dimensions and Contributions of the Arts

Competence, Sharing, Individuation, Goal-Setting, Challenge, and Self-Change

As music teacher and as cultural arts coordinator at Nassau Boces Elementary, my hopes are to continue to present the finest in music, dance, art, and theater to the special-needs children so that they can find their own voices for creative expression. These children are very gifted and need an outlet and recognition for their talents, which may not be academic. The arts will enhance all aspects of their learning.

• Lesson Assessment— + = Frequently, / = Evident, o = Developing

• Students will show in whatever medium they choose to demonstrate to the teacher their understanding of the *Nutcracker* by Tchaikovsky. They could sing, they could play an instrument, they could draw a scene. Expectations are individualized to each student, and praise is given to all as the utter success of the six weeks of lessons culminated in an inspiring musical experience for the students at the Nassau Boces Elementary Program.

Let's Talk About the Positive: Autism

The Autism Society of America, established in 1965, serves the needs of individuals with autism and their families through advocacy, education, public awareness and resources. Three of the most commonly asked questions are answered through public information:

What Is Autism? Autism is a developmental disability that typically appears during the first three years of life. It is the result of a neurological disorder that affects functioning of the brain. Autism is four times more prevalent in boys than girls and knows no racial, ethnic, or social boundaries. Family income, lifestyle, and educational levels do not affect the chance of autism's occurrence.

Autism interferes with the normal development of the brain in the areas of reasoning, social interaction, and communication skills. Children and adults with autism typically have deficiencies in verbal and nonverbal communication, social interactions, and leisure and play activities. This disorder makes it hard for them to communicate with others or become independent members of the community. They may exhibit repeated body movements (hand flapping, rocking), unusual responses to people, unusual responses to attachments to objects, and may resist any changes in routines. In some cases, aggressive and/or self injurious behavior may be present.

The Autism Society reports that it is conservatively estimated that nearly 400,000 in the United States today have some form of autism. It's prevalence rate places it as the third most common developmental disability, more common than Down's syndrome.

Is There More than One Type of Autism? Autism is often referred to as a spectrum disorder, meaning that the symptoms and characteristics of autism can present themselves in a wide variety of combinations, from high functioning and mild to severe.

Parents may hear more than one label applied to the same child: autistic-like, learning disabled with autistic tendencies, high functioning, or low functioning autism. Individuals with autism may have other disorders that affect the functioning of the brain, such as epilepsy, mental retardation, or genetic disorders, such as Fragile X syndrome. About two-thirds of those diagnosed with autism test in the range of mental retardation.

What Are the Most Effective Approaches to Autism? Experience has shown that individuals with autism respond well to a highly structured, specialized education program, tailored to the individual needs of the person. A well-designed intervention approach may include some elements of communication therapy, social skill development, sensory impairment therapy, and behavior modification delivered by autism trained professionals in a consistent, comprehensive, and coordinated manner. The more severe challenges of some children with autism may be addressed by a structured education and behavior program which contains a 1:1 teacher to student ratio or small group environment.

For further information about autism, Asperger's syndrome, other developmental disorders and internet links, please contact The Autism Society of America, 7910 Woodmont Avenue, Suite 650, Bethesda, Maryland 20814-3014, ph: 1-800-3 AUTISM and website: *http://www. autism-society.org.*

Comments from a Special Education Music Teacher
Should you have an autistic student in your music program, the individual may exhibit some of the following traits: Difficulty in mixing with other children; resistant to change; inappropriate laughing and giggling; no real fear of dangers; little or no eye contact; unresponsive to normal teaching methods; sustained off play; apparent insensitivity to pain; echolalia (repeating words or phrases in place of normal language); prefers to be alone; aloof manner; may not want cuddling or act cuddly; spins objects; noticeable physical overactivity; tantrums—displays extreme distress for no apparent reason; not responsive to verbal cues; acts as if deaf; inappropriate attachment to objects; uneven gross/fine motor skills (may not want to kick ball but can stack blocks); difficulty in expressing needs; uses gestures or pointing instead of words.

"Teaching autistic students is fascinating. The students are often very musically gifted, with near or perfect pitch, with the ability to learn even the challenging by rote and repetition. The opportunity to work with a student with autism is an opportunity for tremendous professional and spiritual growth. In many cases the sensory impairment—unusual reactions to physical sensations such as being overly sensitive to touch or under-responsive to pain are balanced out by enhancements in sight and hearing" (Elise S. Sobol, NYSSMA Chairperson Music for Special Learners, music teacher, Nassau Boces Elementary Program, North Bellmore, New York).

Let's Talk About the Positive: ADHD and ADD

One of the most fascinating special learners is the child with autism, but one of the most challenging, difficult, and rewarding special learners are those who are diagnosed with attention deficit disorder or attention deficit hyperactivity disorder. The distinction between ADHD and ADD is as follows: A student with ADHD has ADD and is hyperactive. This means he or she finds it very difficult to sit still and tends to wiggle, fidget, and squirm a lot. Hyperactive people have an incredible amount of energy and are always on the go. A student with ADD has trouble paying attention and concentrating. The command center of the brain, which tells other parts of the brain what to pay attention to and what to ignore, does not work completely on target. There is a neurological inefficiency and chemical imbalance in the parts of the brain that control impulses, sensory input, and focusing of attention. Sometimes the brain of a person with ADD fails to tell the other parts of the brain what to ignore so that a person with ADD might think listening to someone tapping a pencil is just as important as paying attention to what the teacher is saying. ADD is usually inherited, but the condition can also come from a brain injury or lead poisoning. So then a student who has ADD is not necessarily ADHD; but a student who has ADHD has the conditions that a student with ADD has and is also hyperactive. It is important to understand that there may be other disorders in the student with ADHD and that all students need to be considered as separate cases. Rather than dwell on the negative aspects of teaching a student with ADD or ADHD, it is of more value to talk about the positive aspects of a student having ADHD.

Comments from a Special Education Music Teacher
With proper classroom techniques to increase attention, improve listening skills, build organizational and study habits, control impassivity, balance excessive activity levels, and develop immature social skills, a music teacher can find his or her ADHD student filled with the following wonderful qualities: qualities of

being accepting, creative, empathetic, energetic, forgiving, gregarious, intuitive, innovative, inventive, imaginative, inquisitive, risk taker, resourceful, resilient, sensitive, and spontaneous. Many of these gifts are seen in extraordinarily gifted and talented personalities. These qualities provide a vibrancy to the music classroom.

[Compiled by Elise S. Sobol, NYSSMA chairperson, *Music for Special Learners.* For further information about learning disabilities please contact: Council for Learning Disabilities (CLD), PO Box 40303, Overland Park, KS 66204 (913) 492-8755 and Learning Disabilities Association of America (LDA), 4156 Library Road, Pittsburgh, PA 15234 (412) 341-1515. The National Information Center for Children and Youth With Disabilities (NICHCY), PO Box 1492, Washington, D.C. 200114-1492 (800) 695-0285, email *nichey@capcon.net* is a clearinghouse that provides free information on disabilities and disability-related issues.]

Teaching Special Learners Critical Thinking Skills

This project is appropriate and adaptable for upper elementary through high school ages. It addresses the New York State Standards in the Arts while using Standards in Language Arts, Science, Math and Social Studies. The composers chosen are just an example of five of the many composers who have championed their circumstances and developed greatness. This project was developed as part of the NYSUT Effective Teaching Program in Critical Thinking, in which I took part at LIU-Southhampton Campus in August 1997.

The stimulus for this project came from the first class that Mr. Mike Gatto and Mr. Alan Bromberg presented on Critical Thinking (NYSUT ETP program). "How wonderful," I thought, "it would be for the troubled youngsters that I teach to see how prominent musicians handled their own particular setbacks, persevered through difficulties, and now have their distinct place in musical history. Aldous Huxley said, "Experience is not what happens to you, it is what you do with what happens to you."

The children I teach music to are aged 5–10 and are recommended to the Nassau Boces Elementary Program as an alternative educational program. All students have multiple social, emotional, and/or learning disabilities. Some of these students come from good caring and educated parents. Some of these students are in foster care, hoping for some loving parent to adopt them. Some students know who their parents are, and some students have little knowledge of their parentage. Some students have siblings to live with, and others have siblings that are sent to different homes. Some students have above-average IQs and others are below average. Some students can go back to the regular district after receiving the support services. Others need sometimes an even more restrictive environment.

What all students have are the same needs in common: to be loved, to be accepted, and to be given an opportunity through trained professionals to succeed to the best of their abilities. Through studying the lives of prominent musicians who have had their own challenges to conquer in their childhood; it is my goal to positively impact the students through music and help them gain strength over their own unique social, emotional, and educational development. With knowledge and skills to interpret the information these students, even at the most primary level, can extend their potential and surmount their difficulties. This project could take up to six weeks. All classes meet twice a week. The end product of the project would be for the students to create their own web of their lives which would be a beautiful testimony to their enhanced self-esteem. On the long term, students would remember and recall when needed, the stories that helped them to grow and to make a positive contribution to the lives of others.

Ludwig van Beethoven

Data presented to children:

- Born: December 16, 1770, Bonn, Germany

- Died: March 26, 1827, Vienna, Austria

- Parentage: Had a very mean drunken father who beat him to force him to practice the piano. Father wanted son to be a famous prodigy like Mozart.

- Childhood: Life for Beethoven was very hard. He began to go deaf when he was only about twenty-six years old. He became gruff and cross. He didn't have many friends.

- Outcome: Despite handicap and his constant financial struggles, Beethoven is considered one of the most important classical composers of all time. His notable works included nine symphonies, "The Moonlight Sonata," and "Für Elise." Despite his total deafness, not being able to hear a note of what he composed, his last composition included "The Ode to Joy" (theme from the Ninth Symphony), a testimony of his triumph and peace at the end of his life.

- Music examples for students to include: "Ode to Joy," "Moonlight Sonata," *Emperor* Concerto, "Für Elise." Excerpts adapted for each class. Students will view insightful video, *Beethoven Lives Upstairs.*

Giuseppe Verdi

Data presented to children:

• Born: October 9, 1813, Le Roncole, Italy

• Died: January 27, 1901, Milan, Italy

• Parentage: Verdi's parents ran a small inn and sold groceries in a little Italian town called Le Roncole. They sacrificed things for themselves in order to buy Giuseppe an old spinet piano.

• Childhood: Giuseppe showed great musical talent. One day, he was putting some notes together to form chords, he found a chord that he liked very much. When he tried to find this chord again, he could not do so, and he flew into a childish rage. He grabbed a hammer and began to smash the precious piano. His father stopped him just in time before the piano was destroyed.

• Outcome: With time Verdi grew out of his childish rages and produced some of the greatest operas ever written including *La Traviata, Il Trovatore, Otello,* and *Aida.* He died a national hero.

• Music examples for students to include: *La Traviata,* Act 1, Scene I; "Grand March" from *Aida;* "Anvil Chorus" from *Il Trovatore.*

W. C. Handy

Data presented to children:

• Born: November 16, 1873, Florence, Alabama

• Died: March 28, 1958, New York, New York

• Parentage: Father was a minister and thought any music outside of the church was sinful.

• Childhood: Family was quite poor. W. C. worked hard at many odd jobs and gave his parents part of his earnings. He saved a portion for himself. W. C. made music himself by humming through a comb wrapped in tissue. He wanted a guitar, saved his money, bought it. His father forced W. C. to take the guitar back. His father insisted that W. C. become a minister, but W. C. never lost his dream of writing and playing music.

• Outcome: One day a cornet player in the circus sold him a cornet. This was the turning point of his life. He played with the Florence, Alabama band then stayed with music through good and bad times. He formed his own band and publishing company. He became blind, but continued to write music to the end of his life. His nickname was "Father of the Blues."

• Music examples for students to include W. C. Handy's two greatest songs: "St. Louis Blues" and "Memphis Blues."

Louis Armstrong

Data presented to children::

• Born: July 4, 1900, New Orleans, Louisiana

• Died: July 6, 1971 Corona, Queens

• Parentage: Parents separated, lived with his mother.

• Childhood: Louis Armstrong struggled against poverty and hard times in his early years. He broke the law at age thirteen by firing a gun to celebrate New Year's Eve. He was sent to jail then to what was called "The Colored Waif's Home for Boys." It was a reform school for boys in trouble. At it turned out, opportunity came to him at the Waif's Home, and he was asked to join the Waif's Home Band, where he learned to play the cornet. He was allowed to leave the home after one year and return to his mother. He quickly became established as the best trumpeter around.

• Outcome: Louis Armstrong is remembered as the Ambassador of Jazz. His nickname was "Satchelmouth," or "Satchmo" for his big mouth.

• Music examples will include Disney songs, Satchmo-style original recordings of "Hello, Dolly" and "What a Wonderful World."

George Gershwin

Data presented to children:

• Born: September 26, 1898, Brooklyn, New York

• Died: July 11, 1937, Beverly Hills, California

• Parentage: Born in Brooklyn of loving parents. Second of four children.

• Childhood: As a young boy he had little interest in school, he loved sports, particularly baseball. He called boys who took music lessons "sissies" or "little Maggies." He had little interest in music, reading, writing, or arithmetic. But this all changed around the age of fourteen when his family acquired a piano. Whole new worlds opened up to him. He surrounded himself with music and became a schooled musician who studied constantly—composition, piano lessons. At fifteen he left school and worked full-time as a "song plugger" playing the tunes of hopeful composers in Tin Pan Alley. He read all he could about the great musical personalities. He learned to play many instruments so that he might further his knowledge of orchestration. Through his incredible hard work, he was soon a published composer and together with his older brother Ira wrote many songs. George Gershwin suffered incredibly with headaches. He died at age thirty-eight of an inoperable brain tumor.

• Outcome: George Gershwin brought jazz to a major level. Famous works include the opera *Porgy and Bess*; "Rhapsody in Blue" (the first symphonic work using jazz music); Concerto in F with New York Symphony Orchestra at Carnegie Hall. The Academy Award Picture *An American in Paris* with Gene Kelly (1951) was set to Gershwin's music.

• Music examples to include: "Someone To Watch Over Me," "Oh, Lady Be Good," excerpts from *An American in Paris,* "I Got Rhythm," excerpts from "Rhapsody in Blue."

Sample Unifying Questions for Study

All students will be divided into cooperative groups, and teacher and teacher assistants will guide each group with the questions. (It must be reiterated that many of these young children have low cognitive abilities and problems in processing. Therefore cooperative groups at times need to be directed by an adult.)

Students will devise a visual organizer in the shape of a five-pointed star and choose five things of importance to remember about each prominent musician. Each group will present their own star.

1. Was your composer born in New York City?
2. Describe the home environment of the composer/performer you studied.
3. What influences effected his childhood and his study of music?
4. Despite challenges, each personality studied is world renowned. What will you remember about the lives and music of the great men of music that we studied?
5. Indicate favorite musical example on your "star." Example stars follow.

Visual Organizers are Arranged in Chronological Order

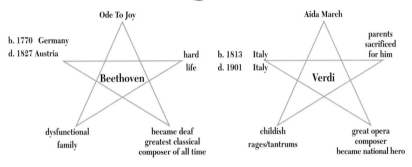

Ode To Joy

b. 1770 Germany
d. 1827 Austria

hard
life

Beethoven

dysfunctional
family

became deaf
greatest classical
composer of all time

Aida March

b. 1813 Italy
d. 1901 Italy

parents
sacrificed
for him

Verdi

childish
rages/tantrums

great opera
composer
became national hero

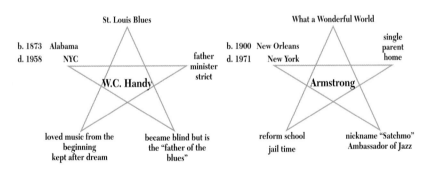

St. Louis Blues

b. 1873 Alabama
d. 1958 NYC

father
minister
strict

W.C. Handy

loved music from the
beginning
kept after dream

became blind but is
the "father of the
blues"

What a Wonderful World

b. 1900 New Orleans
d. 1971 New York

single
parent
home

Armstrong

reform school
jail time

nickname "Satchmo"
Ambassador of Jazz

Someone To Watch Over Me

b. 1898 Brooklyn, NY
d. 1937 Beverly Hills

Supportive
family

Gershwin

disliked school, loved sports
collaborated later with
brother

influential jazz composer
influenced by classical,
theater and movie

Conclusion

Each student will devise their own "star" about themselves.
1. One point will have favorite song.
2. One point will have their birthdate and place.
3. One point will have something about their parentage.
4. One point will have something about a difficulty or disability.
5. One point will have something about an aspiration or
   ambition. I want to be . . .

This project will be used in the music classes this fall at the Nassau Boces Ames Elementary Program. Follow-up activities for these young children will include studying contemporary musicians in the rap, pop, folk, rock, and fusion styles. Further study will also include looking at famous musical stories and their characters creatively thinking critically about the life of Peter and the Wolf, Hansel and Gretel, Peer Gynt, and Billy the Kid. The focus in all cases will be to key into problem solving so the students find in fact and fiction how many ways there are to look at a situation and how many ways there are to solve a problem. In all cases the students will organize the facts by making a timeline or web or other visual organizer. In the end through this process, wisdom will be gained and the best lesson they could learn from the music room is, "Although I have such and such a problem, I can still become . . . I want to be remembered as . . ." This project can be taken and adapted to special learners of all ages. Three quotes to interpret on the higher level would be:

> "Any composer's writing is a sum of himself, of all his roots and influences."
> Leonard Bernstein, composer

> "Success is not success if it affects personal attitudes."
> Ira Gershwin, songwriter

> "Do what you can, with what you have, where you are."
> Theodore Roosevelt

International Speeches

Communication through Music—A Language beyond Words

Elise S. Sobol, Presenter; The ABI/IBC 26th International Congress on Arts and Communications; The Ritz Four Seasons Hotel, Lisbon, Portugal; July 15, 1999.

Good morning. Last night's gala concert included me performing *Ten Variations on an Air of Gluck,* by W. A. Mozart and an arrangement of Cole Porter's *Night and Day.* Being a music teacher for special learners, these two composers can be heard from a different perspective. They each faced extreme challenges in their lives. Mozart, supremely gifted, had a childhood which was spent performing and living "on the road." By biographical accounts, he was a sickly, frail child who suffered from vague diagnosis and questionable treatments. When Mozart wasn't traveling, he was ill. It was a vicious cycle, all of which contributed to his many life difficulties, his kidney failure and early death at age 35.

Cole Porter on the other hand represents another kind of genius. He kept his extraordinarily painful disability from a horseback riding accident from his adoring public. He loved traveling, especially the *fado* (folk art) of Portugal and the country's many famous windmills. But frequently, due to physical pain, his friends would have to carry him when he couldn't use a wheelchair or the support of his canes.

At the Board of Cooperative Educational Services of Nassau County, in Long Island, New York, where I am employed as a music teacher for children with special needs, the children have extreme social, emotional, psychological, behavioral problems with learning disabilities Their age range is 5–10. My most important function is to bring them to a happy place in music where they feel safe, secure and successful. These children need assistance to help themselves find a place of peace when they feel bad, angry, hurt, troubled or sad. Some of the children are from good homes; some of them have no homes and live in a residential facility; some know their parentage, some do not. Some are born with chemical imbalances due to prenatal drug or alcoholic conditions. Some are born with health impairments which interfere with them having a regular routine. Some have inoperable tumors, some are fighting terminal illnesses. But all of these children are someone's son or daughter; someone's hopes and dreams. They deserve to be loved and given every opportunity to develop this potential.

For students with shattered lives, it is important to show that life is full of beauty. This is demonstrated by introducing to them the music of past civilizations when for instance the universe was considered to be a world in tune with harmony. For the Chinese, music expressed a celestial order. For the Indian, all things come from one sound entering both realms of the spiritual and the material. For the Greeks, music contributed to good health curing illnesses of both mind and body. Great civilizations rise and fall but are all connected by the universe—uni (one) vers (song). All children heard their mother's heartbeat in the womb. They heard summer night noises, mountain springs, spring rain, and ocean waves. In my classroom, as a beginning study in the beauty of life, the students have a chance to play replicas of ancient instruments while hearing sounds of nature. This begins to form a sound bank of good, calm sounds where energy can be refocused; where the student can begin to feel sunshine and warmth and not be afraid of the dark. (Demonstration includes use of acoustic relaxation machine and instruments.)

For the children who have been in and out of foster homes, awaiting the possibility of adoption the song "The Earth Is My Home" gives to them a sense of belonging, purpose and plan of action. Please follow me in singing this song with sign.

The Earth is my home.
The Earth is my home.
The Earth is my home.
I promise to keep it healthy and beautiful.
I will love the land, the air, the water, and all living creatures.
I will be the defender of my planet
United with friends.
I will save the Earth.
(Kids for Saving Earth Worldwide, 1991)

Special learners can see a world of wonder challenging us to extend our own human potential. The artist Sarah Perry (1995) marvelously illustrates this wonderment in her book *If* . . . Five examples from this book are, "If frogs ate rainbows; If kids had tails; If toes were teeth; If ugly were beautiful" (and the reason why I purchased the book) "If music could be held" (Seen on overhead projector).

For me, music can be held. Listen for a moment to the following selection of George Hamilton Green's *Triplets*. The xylophone soloist is

Evelyn Glennie who is considered the world's greatest percussionist. Evelyn Glennie is deaf. She is quoted as saying, "My deafness is something unique and I treasure it and I don't want it to be taken away. I want to stay as I am. Sometimes, it has even helped me" (Feb. 1994, *Parade* magazine). Ms. Glennie is the perfect segue for me to teach my students about the life and works of Ludwig van Beethoven and his struggles to deal with not only his abusive home life but later a life of increasing deafness. The tool which I use is the tuning fork. This way my students can hold the music (feeling of vibrations) and are empowered by their new understanding of the past and the present.

Another example of how music can be held is through the beauty of the voice of international singer Andrea Bocelli. Listen to the richness of his gifts in *Canto Della Terra*. Andrea Bocelli is blind. His voice brings to my mind the words of Helen Keller who accomplished greatness despite being deaf, blind and mute. She said, "When one door of happiness closes, another opens; but often we look so long at the closed door that we do not see the one which has opened for us."

Often a child's voice needs to be opened up, having been closed by emotional trauma. The song, "Everybody Has Music Inside" (Greg & Steve, 1980, Youngheart Records), is a song which helps to accomplish this. Please join me in singing this song, "Everybody has music inside, especially for you. Don't be afraid to let it out. It isn't hard to do. You don't have to be a virtuoso, it doesn't matter if you sing just so-so. It's a feeling down inside your soul so come on. You can do it! Everybody has music inside so let a song ring out. Just let it come right from your heart. That's what it's all about. Music is the sound of life reaching out for love. Everybody has music. Everybody has music. Everybody has music inside."

One of my private piano students gave me a coffee mug which had printed on it: "A hundred years from now it will not matter what my bank account was, the sort of house I lived in, or the kind of car I drove, but the world may be different because I was important in the life of a child." That special day came to me one morning in May. On the recent New York State writing tests for fourth graders, there was an essay question to tell about the person you look up to as a hero or heroine. I was shown that one of my learning disabled students wrote the following, "She is the music teacher here, I look up to Ms. Sobol . . . she ask me to get on the drums and she said I was good, after that I play and play and play." (I. Robinson, 5/99).

See with your soul, hear with your heart, touch with the gifts that you have each been given.

It Depends upon Y.O.U.

Elise S. Sobol, Presenter; 27th International Millennium Congress on Arts and Communications; Washington, D.C.; July 2–9, 2000. Education & Culture Seminar.

Greetings and good morning everyone. You will recall that last summer in Lisbon, Portugal, my presentation was entitled "Communication Through Music—A Language Beyond Words" and my closing comments were for you to "See with your soul, hear with your heart, touch with the gifts that you have each been given." Today's message, which has developed from my daily experience with working with a diverse group of socially, emotionally, psychologically learning disabled students, is a message designed to raise your level of understanding about for many, a hidden aspect of social consciousness. Through my work, I've seen that "inside each and every child is a perfect human soul with unlimited potential locked up needing to be set free to find his/her ultimate power of expression" (PTA and Cultural Arts at the Jerusalem Avenue Elementary Program, E. S. Sobol, Feb. 2000). This message transcends all educational systems and it transcends all cultures. For many of the special needs and gifted children throughout the world, studying the creative cultural and musical arts process provides important breakthroughs in academic progress. More importantly, my work has shown me that it is not the child who suffers the disability but metaphorically, it is us—it is our denial, discomfort, fear, intolerance, misinformation, pride, and prejudice. It is our blindness that hides truth and beauty. It is our ears that do not receive the processed message. It is our hands that need a guided strength.

Two recent current events demonstrated those attitudes which I live and teach. The first was the experience of hearing Bruce Springsteen singing to tens of thousands of people at Madison Square Garden his new ballad entitled "American Skin (41 Shots)." His was a voice of social conscience. The audience silently listened with respectful intensity. The troubadour used his position to make a statement to the masses about a very uncomfortable topic. The second experience was the Harvard

University graduation address of Brooke Ellison. This young woman at the age of ten was hit by a car, paralyzing her from the neck down. No one expected her to live but she has, dependent on two things—a respirator and the undivided care, support and attention of her mother. Her message was one that I know well, no one of us knows how life will unfold but miracles do happen. For these miracles one needs only to look at the people in your lives in order to see them (*NewsDay,* June 14, 2000).

I am extremely fortunate that I see miracles daily in my teaching job at the Nassau Boces Elementary Program in North Bellmore, New York. I teach classroom, chorus and instrumental music to students age 5–10 whose problems are so severe that they need alternate placement outside of their regular public schools. These children have shown me how much they can make a difference in the quality of lives of others. They are true messengers of life's wisdom. To start my audio-visual presentation, I have brought to you a performance of the Irish tenor Ronan Tynan, singing a beautiful ballad by Phil Colter entitled "Scorn Not His Simplicity." This was taped live during the Channel 12 TV, Long Island premiere. Mr. Tynan dedicates this song to those who are blessed to have a mentally or physically challenged child in their lives. As many of you are aware, Ronan Tynan was one of those children and now we can all benefit by knowing about his life as a physician and singer. Following this video-clip you will see a select group of 25 children that I teach, performing one of my original songs "We Proudly Sing in Honor of Dr. King." This group of 25 wanted to participate in a countywide competition to show their understanding of the universal ideals of nonviolence, peace, brotherhood and love that Dr. Martin Luther King Jr. dreamed of living. The lead singer is Jamal, an autistic 8-year-old whose very being demonstrates these truths to us. Next are 50 of my students who chose to participate in performances for Long Island's Very Special Arts Festival. This was one of the few opportunities these students have to mingle with the public in a community festival which features their abilities! The students represent a cross-section of the severe and multiple handicaps serviced by the Nassau Boces Elementary Program. Rejoice with them as they sing "This Little Light of Mine."

Now it is your turn. It is one thing to recognize the message I am giving but it is another matter to put it into practice. Please join with me and my students as we sing a song from a musical play by John Higgins and John Jacobson "How Does You Garden Grow?" (1997 Hal Leonard Corporation, all rights reserved). We performed this play in March. Over two hundred special children were involved in the production. The photograph you see was a gift from my students. Each child singing in the photograph is considered mentally challenged. They are dressed as garden vegetables and have important questions to ask you so that your garden of life can fully bloom. (Words overhead.) "Inside each and every child is a perfect human soul with unlimited potential locked up needing to be set free to find his/her ultimate power of expression. but it depends upon your own understanding. It depends upon Y.O.U."

Chime (Big Ben). Thank you for your attention and participation.

Joining in a Common Hymn

Elise S. Sobol, Presenter; 28th International Congress on Arts and Communications; St. John's College, Cambridge University, Cambridge, England; July 19, 2001. Education & Culture Seminar.

Good morning and welcome to the Music Room. There are three rules that we need to follow:

1. Sit in the designated seat.
2. Ask before you touch.
3. Try your best.

Any questions so far? Great.

It is with particular delight that I accepted the invitation to address our international delegation here at St. John's College. Since this is the third Congress I am addressing, this morning's presentation will be a continuation of speaking about my attitude and approach for teaching music to special learners and its universal applications for daily living. On Long Island, New York, my day to day teaching is with students, ages 5-10 who have severe social, emotional, psychological, and behavioral problems with learning disabilities. Their common cases show their lives shattered, oh too many times, at such a tender age. Through music, I can build for them a world that has wonder and beauty and which serves as a foundation for their education to strengthen their successful generalization of information in language arts, science, social studies, mathematics, movement education and the creative cultural and performing arts.

In Lisbon, Portugal at the 26th International Congress, my presentation was entitled, "Communication Through Music—A Language Beyond Words." This presentation so inspired one of our delegates, Dr. Ulf Sunblad, that he wrote a poem to me which he read during the question and answer session following the presentation. The poem was called "Universum." Its translation was printed in the June ABI Newsletter. (Show on overhead transparency original poem by Dr. Ulf Sunblad, July 15, 1999.)

UniVerse (One Song)

All world
Is united
In a common hymn,
Uni verse
Song of winds
Heard in
Trees and waters.
That's why
I love the world,
It sings
In air, in wood, everywhere
And all
Created beings
Know that tune.

Dr. Sunblad asked me to set this poem to music. With careful thought, I have composed the music for this important text. It is sung by the Swedish singer Lillemor Klang Zakkay. Let's listen. (Play recording—Elise Sobol, composer/keyboard/recorder/strings.)

As educators, how can we reach certain disadvantaged or disabled children to make them responsible citizens in a global community? For me, the answer lies in teaching in a reality based system, in a multi-sensory mode. Last summer in Washington, D.C., at the 27th International Congress, my presentation was entitled, "It Depends upon Y.O.U." Y.O.U. is your own understanding that inside each and every child is a perfect human soul with unlimited potential locked up, needing to be set free to find his/her ultimate power of expression. To demonstrate, I'd like to share with you two key elements to my success for teaching music to special learners. One is in the use of the universal colors green, red, and yellow. The second is in the application of the universal shapes of circle, square, triangle and rectangle.

(Show transparency of traffic signal.) Before you is a stop light. On the open road, red means "Stop," yellow means "Caution," and green means "Go." On the open seas, sound and light signals are used to communicate directions. All military personnel understand these signals for navigation. Applying this principle to the music room, the teacher can establish directions for classroom structure. Sound signals are based on the way we speak. Red is the "low" tone and green is the "high" or "Go" tone.

Examples: *Please stand up=low, low, high—red, red, green.*
 Please sit down=high, high, low—green, green, red.
 Adding our middle tone, yellow color, we say:
 Please get in line=high, high, middle, low—green, green,
  yellow, red.
 To bring closure to class by playing:
 Good job=high, low—green, red.

Another classroom management technique is called "The Stoplight Exercise," authored by Daniel Goleman in his book, *Emotional Intelligence* (Bantam Books, NY, 1995):

RED LIGHT: 1. Stop, Calm Down and Think Before You Act.
YELLOW LIGHT: 2. Caution. Say the problem and how you feel.
  Set a positive goal. Think of lots of solutions.
  Think ahead to the consequences.
GREEN LIGHT 3. Go Ahead and Try the Best Plan.

It is remarkable that in nature these three colors are most prevalent. Let us look at a beautiful Lobster Claw Heliconia plant found in the rainforest

in Peru. (Show overhead.) Here the bold red, yellow and green coloring is to attract birds and insects for pollination. Its extreme opposite in nature is exemplified by the poison arrow frog—red symbolizes "Stop" to its predators—"Stop, I am toxic!" Since our Congress is in England, it is interesting to note that the color scheme of red for "Stop" and green for "Go" originated in the British railway system; then it was adopted around the world.

Besides colors we have shapes which can give our challenged youth foundations for lifelong learning. Underneath all of your chairs is a shape. Please join me in some fun while we play the Shape Game. (Source: Greg & Steve, "We Live Together Series, Volume 3," Youngheart Records, 1987.) Now let's go on the road again and look at the information signs for riders and drivers. Identifying now from a new perspective you see that these signs are rectangles, squares, circles and triangles which use red, green and yellow colored signs, plus black on white for absolutely non-negotiable facts. Each shape stands for a direction (show examples) and serves as a signal for cognitive understanding, acting as a guide for civilized behavior among people and nations.

This and more on my attitude and approach to teaching music to special learners is elaborated in my book of the same name, soon to be published. It is a compilation of experience gained through my years of teaching based on the belief in the unlimited potential for learning in all children.

When we listen to a song, the left brain basically attends to the words, the right brain attends to the melody and the emotional center of our brain, or the limbic system, becomes engaged. Our musical intelligience actively involves our whole brain, and because of this phenomenon one can link learning in every activity, culture, or continent to our other intelligences through music. Though the topography, geography and languages may be different, what is consistent are the sounds of nature and man's expression of such. When we study how each creature, land or sea, sings its own song, we learn that this music can blend together in complete harmony.

I love my work, and it continues to show that there is an immortal spirit with full capacity to learn in each and every child, regardless of their disability. In 1841, Laura Bridgman, the first deaf and blind person to learn to communicate through language, proved this at the Perkins Institute for the Blind in Massachusetts. Helen Keller followed, confirming this to future generations of the world. She wrote that "Optimism is the faith that leads us to achievement. Nothing can be done without hope and confidence."

And as I said before, and is worth repeating, "Great civilizations rise and fall but we are all connected by the universe: uni (one) verse (song)." Let us make a difference in the lives of the future children of the world. Let us join together in this common hymn, "Universum." (Play ending of E. Sobol music to U. Sunblad's text.)

Thank you; it was **wonderful** speaking with you again this morning! Enjoy your day!

Professional Articles

Music Success for Special Learners

Special education students can play a vital part in the enrichment of performance groups and general music classes. There is no greater lively art than music for bringing out the learning potential of a student. Dealing with cognitive and affective functions, music provides language for communication and development of self-expression.

A physically handicapped person who may be limited in certain areas can be given the opportunity to excel in the performing arts. A learning disabled person with language skills below grade level can be taught to read music as a foundation skill for literacy. A socially and emotionally immature student can focus his or her attention on suitable instrumental instruction such as drum set which not only builds confidence but may earn the approval of his peers as well.

It cannot be overemphasized that miracles of the human spirit are ever present in the mind and body of a severely handicapped person. Whether the individual is physically, mentally, emotionally or socially handicapped, music is soothing and provides a key for teaching progress in daily living.

Everybody has Music Inside (Greg Scelsea and David Kirschner, "We All Live Together," Vol. 3, Youngheart Records, 1980) is a lively and upbeat song for all ages that reminds us that "music is the sound of life reaching out for love." To amplify this life sound, Janice Buckner in *One Light, One Earth* (Moonlight Rose Publications, 1991) sings:

> One Light, One Earth
> Our chance to shine and to inspire,
> One Light of Hope
> Our chance to live our heart's desire.

Special children, special gifts,
So much that we can share,
We light the way for one another,
And spread love everywhere.

One Light, One Earth
Our voices raised we spark each other,
One Light, One Earth
Our dreams we share with one another.

Making all our dreams come true,
Our special gifts we give,
Challenges we bravely meet,
Teaching what we live.

One Light, One Earth
Our tiny lights they join as one,
One Light, One Earth
Burning brightly as the sun.

A light of truth, a light of hope,
A light of unity,
A light to tell the world we're here
Special, you and me.

One Light, One Earth
Our chance to build this dream together.
One Light, One Earth
Our chance to make it last forever.

Singing, standing, side by side,
Our light, it's burning bright.
We light the earth, we light the sky,
Together you and I,
Together, you and I, burning bright,
You and I, in the light, you and I,
One Light, One Earth.

Music is language beyond words. It is mathematics in process and progress. It is the science of sound and a study of history and cultures. It is architecture of form and geometry of design. Music is an essential part of healing, giving power to the will to succeed.

Whether the least restrictive environment is a regular classroom or a center-based special education program, special learners challenge us to extend our human potential which can, in turn, enable our special learner to reach his or her level of excellence.

Art, Mind and Brain: A Cognitive Approach to Creativity (1982) and *Frames of Mind: The Theory of Multiple Intelligences* (1985) by Howard Gardner are two books which explore our human potential. "Music can serve as a way of capturing feelings, knowledge about feelings, or knowledge about, the forms of feelings." (Gardner, *Frames of Mind,* New York: Harper & Collins, 124). MENC President Dorothy A. Straub wrote in the *Music Educators Journal* (Jan. 1994) about extremes in music educational programs across the country. She stated, "It is incumbent on us as music educators to raise the awareness of the American public about the importance of music and the other arts in our lives and in our schools."

In addition to the National Coalition for Music Educators, the Music Educators National Conference (MENC), the National Academy of Recording Arts and Sciences, and the National Association of Music Merchants; the New York State School Music Association is an excellent resource for music and classroom teachers. Teachers can avail themselves of significant chairpersons and hot-line numbers to work together to strengthen their teaching, assessment, and evaluation programs for all involved.

Music can be used to change behaviors. Music therapy programs can make a difference for people with mental health needs, developmental disabilities, certain injuries, physical disabilities, and chronic illnesses. The National Association for Music Therapy and the Association for Music Therapy can give further information on the healing aspects of music in addressing the physical, psychological, cognitive, and social needs of the students we teach.

In February 1994, the U.S. Senate passed new standards in music education—Goals 2000. This includes music in the list of core subjects along with science, English, history, geography, and mathematics. It is important for the public school educator to realize that every student has an individualized style of learning whether that student is labeled "special needs" or not. AFT President Albert Shanker urged, after calling for a moratorium on full inclusion (15 Dec. 1993), that classrooms need to re-focus on education, on what is best for all children, not to succumb to financial and social policy pressures at the expense of children. MENC's "World's Largest Concert" (Mar. 1994) featured the song "We Are the Children." The words remind us that what we need to do is work together hand-in-hand. Our children stand for goodness and love. They are our future.

We in music can make a daily difference in the quality of our students' lives. Whether a student is in a special educational setting and lucky enough to have music twice a week with additional time for vocal and instrumental instruction, or whether the special education student is mainstreamed in a program that alternates physical education with music, special learners with a teacher who is trained in assessment and evaluation techniques can have music success. This kind of success influences the social and emotional development of all students and improves the quality of music education and performance for all.

Music and the Mouse

Computers are used daily in the Learning Center at the J. Lewis Ames Program for students with learning, behavioral, and developmental difficulties. The students are adept at the new technology and easily adapt to programs with increasing challenges.

When the computer is brought into the music room, technical skills are combined with an active mouse that helps students develop their skills of auditory and rhythmic discrimination. Self-confidence is built while exploration and creativity are fostered. Persistence is rewarded with success. Brought to another level, students can improvise their own musical patterns on acoustic instruments in conjunction with the musical computer programs.

The Thinkin' Things Collection I (Edmark Corporation, c. 1994) has two educational programs that can be used to advantage with autistic, hyperactive, visual, and hearing impaired as well as with slower learners. The two programs are called *Toony Loon* and *Oranga Banga*. *Toony Loon* is melodic and *Oranga Banga* is percussive. Both can be used with Windows (DOS) and the Macintosh systems.

Toony Loon features learning opportunities to develop auditory discrimination of pitch; it strengthens the memory and the ability to sequence. It creates patterns, remembers and repeats patterns and develops creativity and musical sensitivity. *Toony Loon* teaches the differences in timbre by showing the same pitch, F' to F", on the xylophone, water glasses, logs, rubber bands, and singing chickens. Used with the acoustic piano in general music class, the students can match pitches, make their own melodies and have *Toony Loon* play their compositions back. Used to develop musical literacy, elementary dictation can be given using appropriate symbols for each class.

Oranga Banga develops memory skills and can be used with visually impaired students by stressing auditory recognition or the hearing impaired by stressing visual recognition. The sounds are exciting: bass drum, crash cymbal, snare drum, wood block, chimes, gong, triangle and cowbell. The lights on/lights off feature enhances the student's listening skills. What starts out in the beginning as a challenging game turns into musical performance at its best in the end for all students in class!

A good teacher consistently offers his/her students constructive criticism so that learning is an opportunity for continued growth. "Toony" compliments—he says to the student, "I'm impressed; You're good at this; Outstanding; Good Work, You're Great!" If the answer is incorrect "Toony" says "Once Again" always encouraging. "Oranga" is equally strong in his comments bringing smiles and laughter with satisfaction.

Without the sophistication of a music lab, the general music teacher—vocal and instrumental—has the inexhaustible resource for success with their special learners with use of the computer in the classroom. The love of learning is combined with the joy of music making and the belief in the value of technology when the mouse is brought to the music room.

The Magic Microphone and Awesome Video Camera

Outside the music classroom, the special learner is selectively mute, traumatized by life's cruelties. In music class, however, performing with microphone in hand, the child is empowered to speak, empowered to sing and empowered to develop the creativity within.

Using the microphone in the music classroom amplifies and builds confidence in an otherwise quiet or silent child. When he or she has the microphone in hand a star is born, and for one fleeting moment, the child feels bigger than big, stronger than strong, and more bright than dull. On center stage, he or she has a focus point through which positive energy can flow. The microphone becomes an important self-help tool. When the child feels like a star, problems don't seem so overwhelming. He or she becomes more comfortable with themselves.

Like the microphone, the video camera is an equally important self-help tool. The students can watch himself perform after the big show. The student is usually delighted and feels special. He is awed and again feels bigger than big, stronger than strong, and more bright than dull.

The microphone and the video camera are indispensable teaching aides for the special learner. They help mold, instill a sense of pride and accomplishment and help show musical talents not usually recognized. These tools are empowering for the education of the child with special needs.

The Red-Green-Yellow Song

Special learners delight in finding success in performing in the general music class on the xylophone, keyboard and drum set. The key to their success, on a most basic level, is color coding. This firmly roots their musical growth, building competence and confidence. On the road, red means stop, green means go, yellow means proceed with caution—and so it can be applied in music to high, middle and low melodic tones; High—green; middle—yellow; low—red. Students can begin ear training on two tom-toms with the Green-Red Song, a study in High and Low (See Example 1). A third pitch is added with the middle tom-tom for the Green-Yellow-Red Song (See Example 2). Work on drums is transferred to xylophone and keyboard for work in thirds and fifths matching the tone of the tom-toms. Students at first will play the songs responding aurally to teacher clues. Then the students will gradually combine ear, and eye coordination to perform without teacher assistance.

This multisensory approach to music education and performance incorporates visual, auditory and tactile feedback. This reading process is developed sequentially to add green, yellow, red notes to the music staff progressing to the musical notation of meter, rhythm, pitch and dynamics.

EXAMPLE 1

Green - Red Song

<u>Example 1</u>

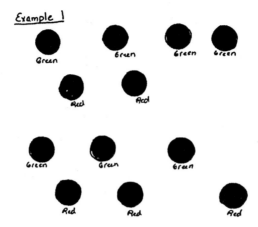

EXAMPLE 2

Green-Yellow-Red Song

<u>Example 2</u>

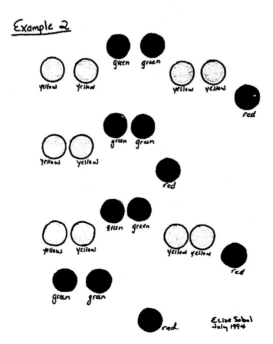

Elise Sobol
July 1994

Assembly Programs

In working with students of special needs, putting on an assembly program meets specific challenges:

- The theme should be something all children can grasp, e.g. Hat Day.
- The assembly program length must be structured to the attention span of the children, e.g. 30 minutes maximum.
- As a large group activity proper behavior needs to be rehearsed in the setting of the place of the program whether by the gym or all-purpose room.
- Each and every student must feel significantly important.
- The music teacher needs to search out the talents of each attending student. Hear what each student says so that student feels he/she is an active participant in the program.
- Each program should feature interesting songs that have an enduring learning purpose.
- Concepts of cooperation, long- and short-term sequencing and memorization should be an integrated part of classroom training for a successful assembly program for special learners.

Loud, Louder, Loudest

Teaching the Dynamics of Life

For the young severely emotionally disturbed student who knows conflict, controversy, and violence, teaching soft, softer, and softest is so necessary for the development of a healthier and socially positive well-being. Asking severely disturbed individuals to play softly on the hand drums or drum set, maracas, or tambourines will so often times draw a blank response. Cognitively these students just haven't experienced soft. In their world of noise, students know screaming and yelling, agitation and anxiety, high amplification with pulsating earth-shattering motion and movement. Silence is not golden. Silence is fraught with the fears of abandonment and rejection. Silence is cold not safely filled with feelings of attachment, warmth, comfort or beauty.

A classroom music teacher is gifted in being able to educate the whole child—his heart, his mind, and his body. Music can provide the forum to guide and enrich a student's life making him capable of expressing the dynamics of life from softest to the loudest.

How can we break through the loud hardened violent skin of a severely emotionally damaged young student? This tough skin has developed in the student as a protection against more hurt. How can we, in a non-threatening way help find points of calm, beauty and safety for these students in music class?

Ed Young in *Voices of the Heart* (Scholastic Press, New York 1997) invites all children young and old to explore the many voices from our heart. The virtuous heart, the shameful heart, the understanding heart, the forgiving heart, the joyful heart, the sorrowful heart, the respectful heart, the rude heart, the contented heart, the despairing heart, the lazy heart, the able heart, the graceful heart, the forgetful heart, the resentful heart, the constant heart, the aspiring heart, the frightened heart, the merciful heart, the tolerant heart, the angry heart, the silenced heart, the evil heart, the doubtful heart and the loyal heart. Mr. Young is an artist, he expresses his thoughts through Chinese characters and visual collage. As musicians we can teach these thoughts through the language of music notation and sound. We can broaden the lives of our students by exposing them to pleasant sound experiences.

What are our soft and pleasant sound experiences that we can bring to the attention of our students?

Let's start with the magical sounds in nature, Tranquil ocean waves offer a sea of tranquillity. Like the fetus in the womb, the protecting waters envelop and bring nourishment to the new life. There is a feeling of safety. Anger and aggression need not be displayed. The winds whistle, the brooks gurgle, the trees sigh, the horses neigh, the cats purr, the frogs croak, and little lambs baa. Quiet little musicians can be found in the tall summer grass waving in the breeze. There are fiddling crickets, buzzing bees, chattering squirrels, squeaking mice and trilling toads. All these are nice sounds, good sounds, pleasant to our ears. These are sounds we should teach our students whether through a walk in the woods or arboretum, or on wonderful sound records that bring nature to our ears. Examples of other non-threatening sounds include those of songbirds—each uniquely expressing their special needs through an ability to sing in musical patterns. Ornithologists have developed memory phrases for us to learn to recognize common songbirds. The red cardinal sings, "hurry home—hurry home" while the bluebird says, "churr-cheerful charmer." The robin's song will remind us to "cheerup-cheerily-cheerup, cheerup, cheerup."

We live in a fast-paced, high pressured, loud society. When we vacation, we try to slow down, unwind from our pressures, and minimize the media impact around us. Whether this is done in a lawn chair in the backyard, or on an island with coconut and palm trees we all need to catch up, rest up and regroup our priorities. A special needs student has difficulty with doing this on even a minimal level. Stresses are magnified and controlling dynamics is next to impossible without assistance. Organically, these students may lack certain balance in their brain functions which cause them to need assistance in training themselves to balance their thinking minds and their feeling or emotional minds in their one brain. Dr. William Glasser, a practicing psychiatrist, psychotherapist and educator says that behavior is "knowledge in action."

The Nassau County Board of Cooperative Educational Services gave Glasser training to all staff in the special educational division. The purpose of this instructional training was to help all students in the program manage their behavior more responsibly. Based on the three-point program described in *Stations of the Mind* (Dr. William Glasser, Harper & Row, 1982) teachers were trained to help their students: 1) understand behavior, both theirs and others; 2) learn and use responsible and effective behavior to make a good and successful life in school; 3) develop social skills that would produce a responsible and successful life in the community. His theory is called Choice Theory developed from the Control Theory of William Powers. Dr. Glasser helps teachers organize their schools into environments that create a better quality of living—ideals of a good life start in the music, math, art, dance, language arts, social studies, science, athletic programs, etc. where a student's physical and psychological needs are interwoven. In their daily activities. Four basic needs should be addressed properly in each discipline.

1) Belonging—students need to be connected to their world. They need to be with people who know and care about them and to know that they are accepted and appreciated. (This is quite hard, for example, when the student in your music class has just been notified by social services that his foster parent is not going to adopt him but is going to adopt his baby sister. How can you expect him to play softly on the drum set?)

2) Gaining Power—a student will grow in knowledge and skill and gain self-esteem through success. Dr. Glasser feels that competence is its foundation; accomplishment is developer and confidence its empowering expression. Through modeling a musical activity, the student will gain power by his successful mastery of same through realistic teacher direction.

3) Having Fun—Having fun improves health, builds positive relationships and enhances thinking. No matter how diverse the students are in the music classroom, activities need to have laughter. The students need to be uplifted and spirited to add to the quality of their successful program.

4) Being Free—all students disturbed, challenged or gifted, mainstreamed or not, need to express control of their own lives. They need to set goals, make plans, choose behaviors, evaluate results and learn from each experience to do things better.

When a student is responsible for making his own good life when things go right, he can feel satisfied and secure. When things go wrong, the student is distressed and needs help to set things right. There are countless examples in newspapers, magazines, radio, television and the cinema about the benefits of music study. To illustrate the good life concept of Glasser, I would like to recall the movie character Gertrude Lang in *Mr. Holland's Opus*. The Honorable Governor Gertrude Lang was ready to give up playing the clarinet in the high school band that Mr. Holland conducted. Try as she might, she felt that she was holding the other players back by her lack of good technique and tone. Mr. Holland would not let her give up. Instead, he realized he needed to apply another teaching strategy for Ms. Lang. Mr. Holland asked Ms, Lang whether playing the clarinet was any fun. He said that music is "about heart, about feelings, about moving people, something beautiful, and being alive . . . It's not about notes on a page."

Then Mr. Holland asked Ms. Lang something personal: what she liked about herself when she looked in the mirror. She replied her hair because her father says it reminded him of the sunset. Mr. Holland then asked Ms. Lang to close her eyes and play the sunset on the clarinet. Ms. Lang let her imagination bring out the music in her soul and it worked!

What do we learn from this? To some it is obvious. To others it is not. Help is needed to supply beautiful images of a sunset, sunrise, colors in the rainbow, swans on a lake. Through music and the sounds of nature we can assist in building up the shattered lives of our special students. Besides the wonderful sounds of nature on recordings, cassettes or compact discs, digital keyboards with their extraordinary sound banks can often experience both hearing the common and the exotic and beautiful. After students have a foundation of the natural harmonic sounds of nature, we can open the doors for active listening experiences with the great music literature.

In summary, music educators can profoundly affect the mental health and welfare of their students by teaching about peace, harmony, beauty, calm, silence, love and laughter. If the environment in the music classroom has the four basic elements of the good life—belonging, gaining power, having fun and being free, then by teaching about the soft sounds of life our students can begin to develop a broad range of dynamics. This repertoire will serve as a key to their success for a better quality of student's inner life. As music educators, we can help our highly charged emotionally disturbed students manage their moods using crescendo and loud for emphasis and decrescendo and soft to show gentleness, kindness and sensitivity. The late Pablo Casals, renowned cellist, humanitarian, and conductor, taught of life through his words and music. "We are one of the leaves of a tree, and the tree is all humanity. A musician, as every man, must take part in the movement of the world."

With these tools our students can separate their aggression with the task at hand and show control of their hands and hearts at the drum set, on the tambourines, and with maracas. Their own storms which rage within can become more self-manageable. With a repertoire of the peaceful sounds of nature, music becomes colorful, not monotone. Through the range of sounds, students will soon be able to successfully play not only loud, louder, loudest, but soft, softer, softest.

The Study of the Arts

Commentary for Public Television, Rochester, New York

The study of the arts spans all educational systems and crosses all cultural boundaries. It is a study of a universal language that bridges similarities in mankind together while celebrating the unique differences. The study of the musical and creative arts *process* enhances cognitive development and therefore is a vital key to all our student's academic progress in the schools, essential to the growth and development of a student's fullest potential. A student, severely challenged, gifted or talented will find that his self-confidence and self-worth is validated through individual and group expression: in music, art, dance or theater. There is nothing quite like the creative and performing arts that develops the use of both right and left brain functions combining the multiple intelligences. The arts bring together tactile, kinesthetic, visual, auditory learning effecting both the cognitive and affective realms. The arts take the abstract and make it concrete spurring the will to succeed.

To insure the success of all students in the arts, it is recommended that teachers apply task analysis for the desired student outcome. A special educator is trained to consider all the steps necessary to teach a song, construct a model, choreograph a dance or stage an act. The goals are realistic to the learning ability of the student. For example some students will be able to do a task with 80% accuracy, 75% of the time. To the special educator, task analysis is a way of thinking and a consistent practice to reach a student. Teacher preparation includes questions such as how to go about achieving the goal and how to mediate the student's response for success. The teacher will then ask in preparation—What does the student need to know or to do in order to accomplish this task? How will I provide a model for the student to work toward mastery? To the special educator this approach makes one see all the different components there are for doing things. It shows the many ways a similar outcome can be reached. It truly includes teaching to the diversity within our schools and for the special learners the approach means breaking down step by step the process even into smaller steps. By consistently teaching the arts in an audio-visual-tactile mode and by concentrating on process not product, even the most impaired can be a full participant in the highest of learning activities. True assessment concentrates on the evaluation of the process of understanding.

For our students, this is the golden key for maturing into responsible citizens in a global community. (February 1, 2001)

Pearls and Roses

From the original thoughts and writings of E. S. Sobol

There is no greater lively art than music for bringing out the learning potential of a student. (1)

My most important function is to bring my students to a happy place in music where they feel safe, secure, and successful. (2)

Dealing with cognitive and affective functions, music provides language for communication and development of self-expression. (3)

Special learners can see a world of wonder challenging us to extend our own human potential. (4)

Music is language beyond words. It is mathematics in process and progress. It is the science of sound and a study of history and cultures. It is architecture of form and geometry of design. Music is an essential part of healing, giving power to the will to succeed. (5)

The general music teacher has the inexhaustible resource for success with the use of the computer in the classroom. The love of learning is combined with the joy of music-making and the belief in the value of technology when the mouse is brought to the music room. (6)

This multisensory approach to music education and performance incorporates visual, auditory and tactile feedback firmly rooting musical growth, building competence and confidence for the special learner. (7)

In putting on an assembly program, each and every student must feel significantly important. The program must have an enduring learning purpose. (8)

The microphone and the video camera are indispensable teaching aides for the special learner. They help mold, instill a sense of pride and accomplishment and help show musical talents not usually recognized. These tools are empowering for the education of the child with special needs. (9)

We, as music educators, have the added capacity to feel and express our emotions directly and deeply. This is part of the creative gifts that we have been given and which set our discipline apart from others. Not only do we instruct the mind but we touch the heart. By caring, by directing, by disciplining, by showing how to be productive musicians we help our students with the tools of life. We plant seeds for self-esteem and determination for the special learner, so he/she can enjoy his/her life to its fullest. (10)

All students challenged, disturbed, or gifted need to express control of their own lives. When a student is responsible for making his own good life, he can feel satisfied and secure. Through music and the sounds of nature, we can assist in building up the shattered lives of our special students. Music education can profoundly affect the mental health and welfare of the students by teaching about peace, harmony, beauty, calm, silence, love, and laughter. (11)

See with your soul, hear with your heart, touch with the gifts that you have each been given. (12)

In Life, you must do that which you are most afraid to do. (13)

Let the Music be your angel wings to carry you through. (14)

Inside each and every child is a perfect human soul with unlimited potential locked up needing to be set free to find his/her ultimate power of expression, but it depends upon your own understanding. It depends upon Y.O.U. (15)

For many of the special needs and gifted children throughout the world, the creative cultural and musical arts will provide this important breakthrough. (16)

Let these efforts serve as a reminder to all that the study of the cultural arts process, music in particular, is a key to lifelong optimism and the academic progress of our students. (17)

For our students, this is the golden key for maturing into responsible citizens in a global community. (18)

References

1. Music Success for Special Learners, *SMN,* March 1995.
2. "Communication Through Music—A Language Beyond Words," Lisbon, Portugal, July 1999.
3. Music Success for Special Learners, *SMN,* March 1995.
4. "Communication Through Music—A Language Beyond Words," Lisbon, Portugal, July 1999.
5. Music Success for Special Learners, *SMN,* March 1995.
6. Music and the Mouse, *SMN,* May/June 1995.
7. Red, Green, Yellow Song, *NYSSMA Notes,* Vol. I.
8. Assembly Programs, *NYSSMA Notes,* June 1995.
9. The Magic Microphone and Awesome Video Camera, *NYSSMA Notes,* October 1995.
10. It Depends on Y.O.U. (Your Own Understanding), *NYSSMA Notes,* Feb. 1997.
11. Loud, Louder, Loudest—Teaching the Dynamics of Life, *SMN,* Dec. 1998.
12. "Communication Through Music—A Language Beyond Words," Lisbon, Portugal, July 1999.
13. 26th ABI/IBC International Congress on Arts and Communications, Lisbon, Portugal, July 1999 said during question and answer session following my presentation entitled Communication Through Music—A Language Beyond Words," July 15, 1999 (The Ritz, Four Seasons Hotel).
14. Teacher to student, in my Melville Studio, August 1999.
15. 27th International Millennium Congress on Arts and Communications, Education and Culture Seminar, July 5, 2000, at The Willard Inter-Continental, Washington, D.C.
16. PTA and Cultural Arts at the Nassau Boces Elementary Program, Newsletter Feb. 2001.
17. PTA and Cultural Arts at the Nassau Boces Elementary Program, Newsletter Feb. 2001.

18. The Study of the Arts, Commentary Provided to Rochelle Cassella, producer for a public television special on the arts, Rochester, New York February 2001.

The *SMN* is the New York State School Music News.

Conclusion

Throughout the pages of this book, I have shown examples of an attitude and approach for teaching music to special learners developed with great joy and fulfillment for enhancing the social, emotional, psychological, and intellectual well-being of my students. Teaching children with special needs has been an opportunity for growth, development, purpose, and service. As a special educator, I've seen that music will reach out with love to heal people of all nations. For children it is the song for the future. It is with this attitude and approach that I share my work as a sincere contribution for others that will follow.

About the Author

Elise Sobol, music educator and concert pianist, has been recognized for her contributions in the field of performance and special education music in the sixth edition of *Who's Who of International and Professional Women,* the Millennium Edition of *2,000 Notable American Women,* and the Ninth Edition of the *International Directory of Distinguished Leadership.* She was also named an Outstanding Woman of the 20th Century by the American Biographical Institute. A special education music teacher for the Nassau Boces Elementary Program since 1988, she teaches children ages five to ten with severe learning disabilities at the Jerusalem Avenue School in North Bellmore, Long Island. Her teaching philosophy is evident in her writings. "Music is language beyond words—Music is an essential part of healing, giving power to the will to succeed. My most important function is to bring my students to a happy place in music where they feel safe, secure, and successful." Ms. Sobol is on the Adjunct Faculty of the Music Education Departments of New York University and C. W. Post College of Long Island University. She is the Music for Special

Elise S. Sobol

Learners chairperson for the New York State School Music Association and on the New York Council for Music Teacher Education Programs. She serves also as the Arts and Humanities Adviser to the Director General of the International Biographical Center in Cambridge, England. Ms. Sobol earned an Associate in Arts degree from Simon's Rock of Bard College, a Bachelor of Arts degree from the New School University with specialized study in piano performance with Murray Perahia at the Mannes College of Music, a Master's of Arts degree in Music Education and Performance from Teachers College, Columbia University, and continues her postgraduate studies in education and neuromusicology, developing materials and methods for enhancing through music the quality of living for the severely challenged. For further information on Ms. Sobol's performance CDs, teaching cassettes, or resource materials, contact *ESSobol@aol.com*.